Pagan Stories for Children:

A Fairy's First Year in the Forest of Songs

by

Shanddaramon

Pagan Stories for Children

A Fairy's First Year in the Forest of Songs

by Shanddaramon

Pagan Stories for Children
A Fairy's First Year in the Forest of Songs
by Shanddaramon

Illustrations by Shanddaramon

First Edition
Published by:
Astor Press
http://www.astorpress.com

ISBN: 978-1-257-75438-0

Produced in the United States of America

The author may be contacted at mail@shanddaramon.com.
For more information visit http://www.shanddaramon.com.

Other Books
by Shanddaramon

For Adults:

1. *Self Initiation for the Solitary Witch: Attaining Higher Spirituality Through a Five Degree System.* New Page Books, 2004.
2. *Living Paganism: An Advanced Guide for the Solitary Practitioner.* New Page Books, 2005.
3. *Dewdrops In The Moonlight: A Book of Pagan Prayer.* Astor Press, 2007.
4. *The Sacred Quest: A Pagan Perspective on the Pursuit of Happiness.* Astor Press, 2008.
5. The Worlds of Tarot: Expanding the Tarot Universe. Astor Press, 2009.
6. Paganism: A Religion for the 21st Century. Astor Press, 2009.
7. Just Being: A Guide to Pagan Meditation. Astor Press, 2009.
8. *The Five Rings: A Guide to Pagan Ministry.* Astor Press, 2009.
9. *Sacred Gatherings.* Astor Press, 2010.
10. *Voices of the Earth: Pagan Songs and Chants.* Astor Press, 2010.
11. *Thoughts on a Pagan Life: Collected Essays.* Astor Press, 2010.
12. *Just Becoming: A Pagan Guide to Discovering and Expressing Your Authentic Self.* Astor Press, 2011.

For Children:

1. *Sabbats of the Northern Hemisphere: A Pagan Book for Children.* Astor Press, 2008.
2. *The Twelve Days of Yule: A Pagan Children's Activity Book.* Astor Press, 2009.
3. *A Pagan Book of ABCs.* Astor Press, 2009.
4. *Pagan Degrees for Children.* Astor Press, 2009.
5. *Pagan Degrees for Children Companion Book.* Astor Press, 2009.

Pagan Stories for Children

Table of Contents

Preface

This book is a collection of sixteen short stories and a prelude that center on the life of one young fairy. Arylide is born and then matures quickly with other fairies in their home called the Great Tree which is located in the Forest of Songs. Each story takes place during or between one of the eight seasonal celebrations: the two equinoxes, the two solstices, and the four days between those events called the Cross-Quarter days. The stories are meant to be both entertaining and educational as they help children learn about the seasonal events and principles basic to modern Paganism.

I was inspired to write the stories after I read Selena Fox's poem entitled "I Am A Pagan." The poem illustrated in very simple terms what it means to be a modern Pagan and I wanted to write a collection of stories that helped to teach those concepts to children in an entertaining way.

My young daughter loves fairies and we often look for fairies in the woods behind our house on Midsummer nights so it made sense to write these stories about young fairies and their adventures in the woods through the seasons. We have a small area of conservation land behind our house and it was those woods that became the backdrop for the stories: the Forest of Songs. There is a small water runoff that leads to these woods and in the early Spring, the runoff can become quite a rushing creek. This became the waterfall that plays an important part in the stories.

One of the main themes that runs through the stories is how Arylide gains her new wings and, eventually, learns about who she is as a fairy in a community of other fairies. Each of the fairies in the Forest of Songs has different colored wings some of which are deeper in color than others. Basic personality characteristics are displayed through theses colors. The inspiration for this concept came from the book I wrote before this one. That book, "Just Becoming: A Pagan Guide to Discovering and Expressing Your Authentic Self" discusses my ideas about personalities and their relationship to the four elements.

The art work in this collection is my own paintings and do not directly reflect the stories but are images that I was inspired to create while writing them.

Mostly, these stories are meant to be fun and entertaining and I hope you and your child or children enjoy reading them as much as I have enjoyed writing them.

Prelude
Welcome to the Forest Of Songs

Image 1: Daffodils

In a quiet neighborhood there is ring of houses that circle a grove of woods. In the middle of the woods runs a tiny creek. Squirrels and other small animals run along the forest floor and among the branches that reach out in all directions. Many birds fly through the air and make nests among the trees. Other animals like deer come in under the cover of darkness to sip water at the creek. At the corner of the woods is a small trickling waterfall that is always more active in the Spring when the snow melts from the long Winter. By all accounts, you might think this is a grove of woods like any other. But it is not. Deep within the woods there live creatures that few people ever see. This is the Forest of Songs; this is the land of the fairies.

In the Forest of Songs, the small trickling waterfall is a grand waterfall and beside it is a large tree called the Great Tree. The tree is tall and proud and it stands over the rest of the woods. Beside it is some smaller but equally proud trees. If you listen quietly in the breeze you can hear the trees talk to each other and to the creatures that come near it. They rarely say much because they really do not like to talk. Mostly, they like to feel the soil and water at their roots and they like to bask in the sun and the rain. Just being a tall tree is often enough for a tree.

In the Forest of Songs, the trees are home to many creatures but the ones who truly love to fly in and around the Great Tree are the fairies. They make their homes on the branches as they flit and fly around being merry and having fun. Fairies are like people only they are much smaller and lighter. Their bodies are somewhat clear and greenish (to stay hidden in the woods) and most have two pairs of colored wings. With these wings, they can hover like humming birds and they can dart between leaves like bees. Though they may do odd jobs around the forest like guide the Autumn leaves to the ground or teach songs to birds, mostly they enjoy having fun, playing jokes, and flying about in the sunshine.

On this bright morning, the forest was filled with dew and mist. It had rained the night before and the rain had melted some of the snow that had filled the floor of the forest for months. In fact, enough of the snow had melted that a few hardy flowers had just pierced through the surface of the snow. Slowly, the mist began to dissipate as the first rays of the sun peeked through the branches of the trees. The golden rays filled the Forest of Songs with bright oranges and yellows that reflected off the browns of the tree trunks and the clear white of the remaining snow.

As the sun rose further, the Great Tree became alive with the sight and sound of fairies. They each rose gently from their leaf nests and tree trunk houses. Usually there were several fairies that flew around and filled the air with color while many others simply enjoyed sitting and chatting or just lying around in the sunshine. But this was not a typical morning.

Image 2: Arylide in the Flowers

On this morning, some new fairies were about to be introduced into the world. In the Forest of Songs the flowers are the cradles that hold the egg of Earth Mother and the rain is the seed of Sky Father. When the snows first start to melt, the hardiest of flowers break through the surface of the ground and reach for the light and warmth of the sun. When they open near the Great Tree, some of the flowers hold within them a small fairy child.

Today was just such a day- for a gentle rain had filled the ground from the previous evening causing most of the snow to melt and the ground to warm. A single daffodil pushed through the ground and started to open. Immediately, several fairies flew down toward the flower. With their wings they fanned the flower with warm air and coaxed it to open its petals. Slowly the flower responded until inside was revealed a small wingless young fairy. Gently, the other fairies peeled back the flower petals until the new fairy was exposed. One fairy picked up the child and cradled it in her arms. Together, the other fairies gathered around the young one fanning her with their wings to keep her warm. They flew up to the Great Tree while some other fairies went down to the ground to find leaves and branches. Together they found a place in the tree to build a nest for the new fairy. They gently placed her in it and then let her rest. Just then a breeze blew across the branches of the tree and a gentle whisper could be heard.

"Arylide," the Tree murmured. "Arylide," the Fairies repeated softly. Thus the fairy child Arylide or Ary was born.

For the next few weeks she would sleep and various fairies would check on her and tend to her. Some placed nectar and sap on her lips to eat while others made sure she stayed warm and comfortable. Over the next few days, the snow slowly melted, the breezes warmed, and the sun rose earlier and earlier every morning. Each day brought more life and strength to the new fairy child. Soon, the child would wake.

Story no. 1
Arylide Meets Amber

Arylide was a young wingless fairy who lived on a branch of the Great Tree at the edge of the Forest of Songs. These are the stories of her first year.

Image 3: The Forest Of Songs

The young fairy child Arylide opened her eyes and stretched her small body. She stood and took her very first full and long breath and peered out from her small nest on a branch of the Great Tree. Below her the rushing water of the waterfall filled her new ears with sound and the mist from its waters created a rainbow in the sunlight. All around the tree, fairies of all shapes and colors flew about. They seemed to be in a state of great excitement but Ary was, as yet, unaware of this. She was only curious about who and what she was.

The first thing that she discovered was that, although it seemed as if all the other fairies around her could fly, she could not. She had no wings. She peered out over the edge of her nest and watched the others fly. They were fast and graceful and elegant. They could turn quickly, rise suddenly, or move from one place to another in the wink of an eye. She wanted to fly. She wanted to feel the air rush through wings but she could not. She found out that she could do one thing, however. She could climb. Her fingers stuck to the bark of the tree and she could easily move up or down the tree at will. So, that's what she did. She climbed.

As she slowly made her way up the Great Tree, she saw many fairies along the way but they were all flying about in great excitement. Some of them stopped to wave hello to her but they all seemed to be in too much of a hurry to say anything. After a while, she saw a large branch and noticed a grand old nest set upon it. She made her way toward it and climbed along the dry branches and leaves to peer over the side. In the nest were branches that were propped up along the trunk and on the branches were lots of books - books of all shapes and sizes. In the middle of the nest was a large flat stone and a smaller stone set beside it. On the large stone were stacks of papers, long bird feathers and jars of a dark liquid. In the far corner she thought she could make out what looked to be a large open book. The whole nest seemed quiet and peaceful. It displayed a sense of ancient wisdom just like the dusty old books that filled it.

Ary was enjoying the feeling the nest gave her and thought she could just curl up in a corner and sleep peacefully on a cushion of leaves. Or, she thought, she could grab one of those books and sit down to do some quiet reading - only she didn't yet know how to read. For a moment she thought about climbing over the edge of the nest when she was startled by a movement. The open book in the far corner started to move downwards until Ary thought she could see a pair of eyes. Ary quickly ducked down below the edge of the nest to hide.

"Come," said a female voice from inside. It sounded like a soft friendly voice but Ary hesitated.

"Come inside little one," said the voice again. "I will not hurt you."

Ary gingerly looked over the edge of the nest. There in the corner with a book in her hands was a yellow-winged fairy. She was old but had an air of elegance and grace about her.

"Come, Arylide," she said. "Come and talk with me."

Ary pulled herself over the edge and stood but was still a little nervous.

"Did you call me Arylide?" she half whispered.

"Why, yes," the yellow-winged fairy replied. "Arylide. That's your name. Ary for short."

"But how do you know my name?"

"We all know your name. It was whispered by the Great Tree when you were born."

"And what is your name?" Ary asked moving slowly closer to the old fairy.

"I am Amber."

"Amber." Ary repeated the name softly. "That's a beautiful name."

"Thank you my dear." The old fairy watched as Ary's eyes darted about the room. She lifted her hand and made a sweeping gesture. "Please. Make yourself at home."

Image 4: Amber in the Meadow

As if to allow Ary to explore without her watchful eyes upon her, Amber lifted her book back up to her eyes and pretended to read. Ary slowly moved about the room and looked around. There were so many books and she had no idea what any of them were about. Everywhere around her were so many words - in books, on pieces of paper, and on various scraps around the nest.

"So many words," Ary spoke softly.

"Words are ideas."

Even softer Ary whispered. "So many ideas."

Amber lowered her book once again. "Once you learn to read you can grasp these ideas yourself."

Ary suddenly looked excited. "Can you teach me to read, Amber?"

The yellow-winged fairy put her book down on a small rock near where she sat. "Oh my," she began. "I am not a teacher. I like to think about things and write down ideas but I do not consider myself a teacher. To learn ideas is one thing but to communicate ideas to others is an art unto itself. But, if you really want to learn to read, I will try to help you. Not today, though. Today is a day of celebration."

"Oh, I see," said the young fairy. There seemed to be so much to take in with this new world. She decided to walk to the edge of the nest and watch all the fairies fly about.

"Amber," Ary said, "What is all the excitement about?"

"Oh, well," Amber piped up. "Today is the Spring Equinox. It is a time to celebrate the awakening of Earth Mother. Today the sun has kissed the cheek of the princess to awaken her from her long sleep and we celebrate. At this time, the light of day and night is balanced. This is when the birds lay their eggs and other creatures have their young. Today Earth Mother paints the world with color so we celebrate with color as well. We help the birds settle their eggs into nests and we even help to color those eggs. We decorate our nests with fallen flower petals and anything else that might be colorful. Some fairies like to hide baskets of food and fun things for others to find. Mostly it's a chance for us to fly about and enjoy the colors and warmth of Spring."

To Ary, the fairies looked like they were having great fun and she wished she could join them but she could not fly.

Amber interrupted her thoughts. "Yes, it's hard when you want to play with them but you cannot. Don't worry, though. You will have your own wings soon enough."

Ary turned toward the elderly fairy and asked, "When?"

"Wings must be earned through acts of kindness."

"How do I do that?"

"Just pay attention and be ready. Chances to help others will always come up but you must be ready to act when they do."

Ary saw the beautiful yellow wings that moved softly behind Amber. Her wings were not as clear as some others and Ary thought that was probably because of her age. Ary turned her attention back to the sky around the Great Tree that was filled with the sights and sounds of flying happy fairies. There were fairies of all shapes and colors and they seemed to laugh in the sunshine as they played and hunted for treasures. She looked longingly at them and watched them for some time until she began to grow tired.

At that time Ary heard Amber behind her moving some leaves and feathers into a corner of the nest. As if Amber had read her thoughts, the yellow fairy began making a small bed for Ary to lie in. When she was done she spoke. "Come and rest. There will be many equinoxes ahead for you. Blessed Season!"

Ary thought about climbing down the tree to reach her own nest but she was tired and felt safe and warm in Amber's nest so she walked toward the soft spot in the corner and fell asleep. She was glad to have made a new friend.

Story no. 2
Arylide's First Act of Kindness

Arylide was a young wingless fairy who lived on a branch of the Great Tree at the edge of the Forest of Songs. These are the stories of her first year.

Image 5: Acorns

It was early Spring In the Forest of Songs and only small bits of snow stubbornly hung on as the days grew increasingly longer and warmer. The early season flowers were in full bloom some of which contained newborn fairies just like Ary had been a few weeks earlier. Warm breezes wafted through the branches of the Great Tree and the fairies enjoyed flying in the warmth and light.

Many times Ary enjoyed gathering with other fairies to have a breakfast of tree sap and leaves. She and other very young fairies had to remain at the Great Tree because they could not yet fly but others could fly to different trees and enjoy the flavors of their seeds and flowers. This morning, however, Ary decided that she wanted to have something different to eat. She had noticed that sometimes other fairies collected nuts and broke them apart to eat the insides and she wanted to know what a nut tasted like. The problem was that nuts were found on distant branches or on the ground and they were hard to crack open. Since it was early Spring, there were still a great deal of acorns that could be found on the Great Tree. She decided to find one and take it back to her nest.

It seemed like a simple idea. All she had to do was go to a branch that had a nut on it, pick off the nut, and then carry it home. Ary soon found out that it was not so simple to do after all. She could easily find a nut but it was not so easy to get it down and grab it. The nut was usually out far on the branch and hung down amid the leaves in such a way that it was hard for her to grab while she still held on to the tree for balance. My! How she wished she could just fly up to the nut and pluck it right off the tree, but she couldn't.

After trying several times to take hold of a nut from a branch, she decided to try something different. She thought that she might be able to knock the nut off the tree and let it fall to the ground. All she had to do next was climb down the tree and scoop the nut up from the ground and then bring it back up to her nest. The idea would entail a lot of climbing but it might work, she thought. She broke off a small twig and then moved as close to the nut as she could.

She swung once, twice, three times toward the nut but missed each time. Finally, she reared her arm way back and tried again and hit the nut where it was connected to the branch. There was the sound of a snap and then the nut hurled to the ground where it landed with a light thud. Ary watched as the nut hit the ground and then bounced and rolled away from the tree trunk. She followed it with her eyes until it stopped against a rock.

Quickly she made her way down the long trunk of the Great Tree and raced toward the ground to retrieve the nut but before she could get to it, a great blue bird swooped down to the ground and snatched up the nut. Ary stopped and could do nothing but watch the bird take away the nut she had worked so hard to get. She let out a sigh of disgust and anger. Ary, however was quickly becoming a fairy that did not give up easily. She decided to try again. So she found another nut on another branch and whacked it off as she had done before. The nut fell to the ground and bounced away into the grass. Ary watched it roll away and before she could even begin to go after it, a small animal popped out of the ground and snatched the nut away.

"Ohhhh!" She cried out. She tossed her small stick that she had used to knock the nut down out and away. It hit another branch and then bounced to yet another branch before hitting the edge of a nest.

"Hey!" cried a voice from below.

Ary heard a pair of wings heading toward her. All of a sudden a brown-winged male fairy appeared directly in front of her and he was holding the stick that she had just thrown.

"What's the idea?" he said angrily. "You almost hit me!"

Ary truly felt embarrassed. "I'm sorry. It's just that I've been trying all morning to get a nice acorn for breakfast and I am not succeeding."

"Well, be more careful where you throw your sticks," he said. "There are others living around here you know." The brown fairy began to fly away with Ary's stick in his hand.

"Careless young fairies, he whispered under his breath as he disappeared.

Ary just sat there silently in the warm breeze and stared out into the forest. She could see branches swaying gently in the wind and she saw several flowers sprinkled throughout the forest floor. For a long time she just sat and sat and sat. She didn't have the determination to try again and she was too tired to do anything else. So, she just sat.

Suddenly the brown-winged fairy appeared before her as fast as he had disappeared only a few minutes ago.

"Well?" he enquired looking directly at her.

"Well, what?" she returned.

"You're not going to just give up are you?"

"As a matter of fact, yes. Yes I am."

Still flying just in front of her, the brown fairy placed his hands on his hips. "Oh goodness," he exclaimed." He flew beside her and sat down.

"You should only give up when it is to your advantage to do so," he began. "Instead of giving up, try a new way."

"I thought I was..."

"Ah, but I was watching you," he interjected. "You were mostly doing the same thing over and over again." In a flash he was off the branch and flew in front of her again.

"Will you come with me?" he asked with his hands out to carry her.

Ary thought it over and then allowed him to pick her up. They flew down a little ways along the tree until they came to a knot in the tree trunk. The brown fairy stopped in front of the hole and let Ary climb in. He followed behind. Ary thought it would be dark and frightening inside but it was not. The walls and several places on the floor contained crystals that glowed a beautiful light green color. The crystals were placed around the room in such a way that they caught and amplified the sun's light. The room was filled with a lot of small items like tubes and boxes and strange devices. After looking around the room, Ary turned toward the brown fairy.

"Who are you?" she asked.

"My name is Russet but everyone just calls me Russ." He noticed her curiousity about the objects in his room. "I like to experiment," he said.

"I see," said Ary.

Image 6: A Squirrel

"Come. Let's take a look at your problem," said Russ.

Russ moved toward a stone table and pushed aside several charts and notebooks and measuring devices. Under a pile of strangely marked pieces of paper he found a clean sheet. Then he searched about and finally found a feather. On a shelf was a bottle with a dark liquid that Ary had seen before in Amber's nest as well. He opened the bottle and dipped the end of the feather into the liquid. Then he began drawing on the paper. Within moments he had sketched the Great Tree and the ground beneath it. Then he drew an acorn on the ground.

"This is the problem, as I see it." Russ pointed to the drawing. "The distance you must travel to find an acorn on the tree and the distance to the ground where the acorn ends up is too great for you to cover in time to stop another creature from quickly grasping said nut."

The brown-winged fairy tapped on the paper with his pen as he talked. Then, he continued: "The obvious solution, of course, is to quickly fly down and grab it before that can happen."

Ary turned her back towards the brown fairy. "But I don't have any wings," she said with hint of frustration.

"Not yet," he corrected her. "This fact, of course, presents us with a greater challenge. However, I have a hypothesis!"

"A what?" she asked.

"A hypothesis. It's a kind of guess on what you think might happen. I think that if you can attach something to the nut before it falls down that you may be able to retrieve it before another creature can get it." Russ was now tapping more wildly on the paper with the ink tipped feather.

To Ary it just looked like a mess but she was willing to try something new.

"Let's try an experiment," Russ called out as he ran towards a corner of his room. From there he dove into a pile of objects. Soon there were all kinds of things flying through the air.

"You never know when you need something, you know. Ah, here it is," he called out. In his hand he held a string of vines. On one end he tied a loop.

"Here," he said to Ary. As she took it from him, he explained. "Toss this end over an upper branch. Lasso the same end of the rope around the top of the acorn and chop the nut from the tree. When it falls, the rope will go with it and you can pull the nut back up to you before something else can grab it." With a little grin Russ finished his speech with: "It's quite a good plan, I have to say."

"Aren't you going to help me?" asked Ary.

"Well, um, no," he replied with some embarrassment. "That wasn't part of the plan, really."

"I see," muttered Ary in disappointment. Ary grabbed the vine rope and started to go outside. She stopped at the entrance and turned around.

"Thanks for the, uh, hypothesis," she said

Just before leaving, she noticed the twig that she had thrown down from before leaning against the wall. She grabbed it and left.

"Sure thing," replied the brown fairy as he returned to his experiments.

Ary looked around on the outside of the entrance to the brown fairy's trunk hole. She looked up to the sky where the rays of the sun shook hands with the opening buds of the Great Tree. She spotted an acorn not too far from where she was standing and headed toward it. When she got near it, she followed the plan as described by Russ. She found a branch above the one holding the acorn and threw the looped end of the vine rope over it and caught it after it had wrapped around the upper branch. She then threw the loop toward the nut. It took a few tries and several grunts of frustration before Ary managed to get the loop over the nut. She pulled the rope until it tightened around the top of the nut. She then took the other end of the rope and tied it down to a branch near her. When that was all done she took her twig and swung several times at the nut to knock it off. Maybe because she had so much practice from before she was able to knock down the acorn after only the second attempt. The nut went sailing to the ground and as it went so it took the vine rope with it. The rope hissed as it worked its way down. Suddenly, there was a thud and a pop. The acorn had reached the ground and the rope had gone taut as it held it tight. The plan had worked! Ary began whooping and hollering.

The combined noises had brought several fairies out in curiosity. They noticed what she had done and they settled down to clap and watch. "Go Ary!" one of them said.

Now came the hard part, Ary thought. She reached up towards the rope that was pulled tight above her. She pulled on it hard and the nut started to move. Slowly but surely she began to pull it up towards her. Several times it got stuck on a branch or piece of bark but she pulled harder to break it free and kept going. The other fairies started to cheer. There came a moment when the acorn got really stuck and it wouldn't budge no matter how hard she pulled. The air got quiet except for the sounds of Ary's grunts and groans. Then, suddenly, there was a rush of sound as the other fairies who were watching rushed to help the young wingless fairy. They all pulled the rope until the nut slowly made its way up to her. Ary grabbed it and pulled it to her while the others cheered.

"Thank you. Thank you all," she said. They all responded with "You're welcome!" and "No problem!" and things like that but in a heartbeat they were all gone. Ary felt the rush of air from the flutter of their wings. It was like a great wind had suddenly whisked them all away. Ary stood and wondered what had happened, when she noticed a sound that came from behind her. It was a loud almost crackling kind of sound and it made her freeze in fear. Slowly she found the courage to turn around. Staring at her from another branch was a squirrel. It was staring at her and the nut. Ary held the nut tight and stepped back carefully on the branch. Within a few steps, yet another crackling sound came from behind her. She turned to see another squirrel looking at her. Before she could even move, yet another smaller and younger squirrel appeared on another further branch.

Ary wasn't sure what she should do. She thought about picking up the twig she had used and swatting away at the squirrels that now surrounded her on all sides but she hesitated. If they wanted to have pounced on her and steal the nut from her they easily could have done just that but they were barely moving at all. Then, Ary started to have a feeling come over her. She relaxed and let the feeling take her and in an instant she felt she understood the squirrels. They had not come to steal the acorn. They were asking Ary if they could have it. As if to confirm her feeling, she turned and looked at each squirrel. All three remained still except for their nervously twitching tails. She then looked at the nut in her hands and thought about all the hard work it had taken for her to get it. She didn't really want to give it up but she closed her eyes and looked within again. Though she was hungry she had not had the difficulties that the squirrels had faced finding food during the Winter. She was hungry but they were more hungry. She knew that she could always find more sap and other food to eat.

Ary let out a deep remorseful sigh and then slowly put the nut down and stepped away from it. The first squirrel looked once at her and then at the nut before swiftly grabbing it and running off. The other squirrels followed quickly behind the first until they were all gone as fast as they had come. She sat down and felt tired and hungry.

"That was a nice thing you did," came a voice from another branch high above Ary. She looked up and saw a pair of yellow wings coming down toward her. It was Amber and she flew down and sat beside Ary.

"What were they?" Ary asked her friend.

"It was a family of squirrels."

"A family?"

"A small close knit group bound together by love," spoke Amber.

"Oh," Ary replied. She fell silent for a moment and then said: "I worked so hard for that silly acorn."

Amber placed a hand on the young fairy's shoulder. "I know you did. I asked some friends of mine to have a couple put in your nest for you."

Ary turned her head toward the older fairy and smiled. "Thank you."

Amber stood up. "Go back and rest and here..." She reached down and grabbed the twig Ary had used. "You'll probably need this."

Ary took the stick and then asked: "Why?" but the yellow-winged fairy had flown off slowly but gracefully. Ary started to work her way down the tree but stopped briefly because her back had suddenly become itchy. She used the twig to scratch the itch.

$\mathscr{S}$tory no. 3
Arylide's Second Act of Kindness

Arylide was a young wingless fairy who lived on a branch of the Great Tree at the edge of the Forest of Songs. These are the stories of her first year.

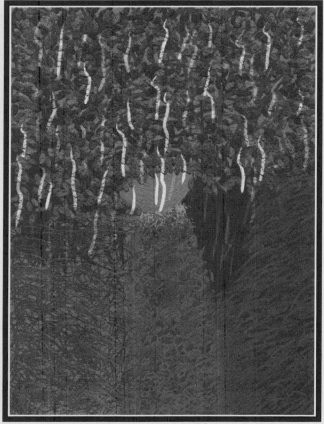

Image 7: The Forest In Ribbons of Color

It was the height of Spring and fairies were everywhere flying and singing around the Great Tree. Ary awoke hearing their songs and was immediately caught up in their excitement. She went to the edge of her nest and looked beyond to watch them. Some were busily collecting seeds and the thin white puffy substance that came from one particular long plant. They collected the white substance and then rolled it into long thin strings. These they colored by crushing berries that were ripe and full in bushes throughout the woods and then they dipped the strings in the different colored liquids. The forest was practically on fire with all the colors of the flowers and bushes and berries. Next, they took the long colored strands and strung them on branches throughout the Great Tree. The effect was stunning. The forest was already alive with color but now the tree was filled with a rainbow of tints and hues as well. Long strands of many shades of colors hung from the branches of the Great Tree and swayed lazily in the warm morning breeze. In the air were also the sounds of the different fairies singing and dancing in the wind.

Ary watched and wished that she could join them. She began to wonder if she were the only wingless fairy in the forest but she knew that other fairies had been born wingless in the flowers and were somewhere in this same tree looking out at the beautiful colors being spun before her.

After watching for a short time, Ary decided to climb her way up to her friend Amber's nest and find out what was going on. Amber was an older and wise fairy who often had answers to her questions. Ary turned and worked her way up the large tree trunk until she reached the yellow-winged fairy's home.

As usual, Amber was sitting in her acorn shell chair reading a book and scribbling notes on various pieces of paper. She barely noticed that Ary had entered her nest. Or, so Ary had thought. The book in front of Amber moved slowly until her eyes were revealed.

"Ah," she began. "My young friend Arylide. What brings you to me today?"

"The same thing that always brings me to you," replied Ary.

Amber put her book and her notes down and looked fully at the young fairy. "And what is it you wish to know?" The old fairy looked around and acted as if she suddenly noticed what was happening. Ary was about to speak but Amber began again. "Ah, wait! Let me guess. You want to know about all the excitement today."

"Yes," replied Ary.

"Well," began the yellow fairy, "let's begin with what you know."

"OK," said Ary happy to be playing a game with her friend. "I see a whole lot of fairies singing and dancing and decorating the tree with colorful strands."

"Good. What does that tell you?"

"There's a celebration of some sort."

"Good," piped Amber. "What else do you know?"

"That's it," she replied.

"Look around you."

Ary looked at the colors: the flowers on the ground, the strands waving on the tree, the bright sunlight, the bright green of the new buds on the trees, and the different colors of all the fairies flying here and there. She inhaled the smells being expelled from all the new plants. She listened to the somgs of all the birds that returned here for the new season.

"Of course," Ary exclaimed. "It's Spring."

"Right again," Amber smiled. "To be precise it's the middle of Spring and it's a day called a cross-quarter. Today we celebrate the rebirth of Earth Mother as she awakes from the long sleep of Winter. We celebrate fertility and growth and we celebrate that growth through song and dance. We also pay tribute to our home, the Great Tree, by filling it full of color and motion."

Ary sat at the edge of the nest and took in the sights and sounds. "It's all so beautiful," she whispered. As she watched, a family of squirrels ran across the branches of a tree not too far in the distance. It made her think for a moment. Then she turned back towards Amber.

"I had another question," She began. "You once told me that animals have families but you have never talked about fairy families."

"It is one of the things that make us different from other creatures. We are born from nature. Earth is our mother and Sky is our father. Sun is our grandfather and Moon our grandmother. We call the fairies who live together in the same place like this tree a clan but we really have no immediate family other than each other and all beings."

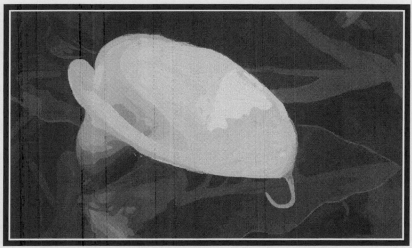

Image 8: A Lily

Ary sat silently for a few moments and thought about what the yellow-winged fairy had told her. Then she turned her attention back to the celebration going on around her. There were fairies of all colors flying in every direction. Some were singing, some were decorating the tree, and still others were just dancing about. Ary's eyes were drawn towards one particular green-winged fairy. He seemed to fly faster than the others and was so active that he appeared to just be a dark blur that often mixed in with the colors of the budding leaves and new grass.

"Who is that?" Ary asked.

"Who is who?" Amber countered.

"The green fairy down there. He's so fast. It's like he dances with the wind itself."

"I suspect you are watching Kelly. He's a very active fairy. He loves to move any way that he can which makes him really good at dancing and playing moving games. There's an easy way to find out if I am right."

"How?"

"Kelly is particularly fond of a certain hard to find mushroom."

"How do I find this mushroom?"

"Well," started Amber with a smile, "it just so happens that I keep some of them here just in case I need Kelly to help me get something moved."

The yellow fairy rose from her chair and moved toward the table in the center of her nest. She reached under it into a small hole and pulled out a small and dark colored mushroom. She walked to the edge of her nest near where Ary was sitting and said: "Arylide, meet..." With those words she tossed the mushroom over the side and when the mushroom had barely left her grasp, the green fairy from below appeared in an instant. "...Kelly," finished Amber. Before she could even blink her eyes, Ary was suddenly looking at the green-winged fairy.

"Pleased to meet you," said Kelly as he managed to both bow slightly and take a bite out of the soft mushroom. Kelly then turned toward Amber. "Hey, Amb. What do you need moved this time?"

"Just wanted to introduce you to our young friend, Arylide."

"Well, it's been a pleasure but I have to..." begins Kelly but he is interrupted by a loud sound. It had come from behind him on a branch not too far away. All of them turned their attention toward the source of the disturbance. Caught between several small branches and some new leaves was a small bird.

"It's a trapped baby bird!" called out Kelly.

Ary could tell that he was about to head in that direction so she called out to him.

"Wait! Take me with you!" she shouted.

Kelly hesitated for a moment but then flew over to Ary and picked her up in his arms. As they flew over, Kelly spoke to Ary.

"You have to keep it calm while I clear the branches that are trapping it." He said.

"How do I do that?"

Together they landed near the bird. It began to panic at the sight of the two fairies. Kelly walked to the side of the bird and touched it gently and closed his eyes. Within a moment the bird started to settle down.

"You have to talk to it," Kelly whispered, "with your mind. Send it comforting thoughts and energies. Come on." Kelly motioned Ary over to the bird.

Ary moved over to where Kelly was standing and placed her hand on the bird. She began to say inside her head things like: "It will be o.k." and "You'll be fine."

As if he could hear her thoughts, Kelly said: "Don't just say it, mean it! Feel it! Say it from your heart!" Ary thought she was doing the best she could already but Kelly continued. "I'm going to raise those branches over there so the bird can get free. You've got to keep it calm or it will only make things worse."

Ary kept thinking calming thoughts while Kelly flew over to the branches that were over the bird and kept it pinned to the tree. He situated himself under the branches and began to lift them. The sound of snapping and cracking that the moving branches made startled the bird and it began to panic again. Ary's concentration was broken and she started to panic as well.

"Arylide!" Kelly shouted.

"I'm trying," she called back.

Kelly was struggling to hold the branches while the bird kept moving and trying to get itself free. "From your heart!" he shouted.

Ary thought about how she truly wanted the little bird to be free. She concentrated on her feelings of compassion within her heart and focused on sending those feelings. After a few moments, the bird began to calm down and Kelly was able to get the branches cleared. The bird moved its head a bit until it was able to look into Ary's eyes then it wriggled itself free and flew away. Ary suddenly had feelings of gratitude come over her mixed with feelings of exhaustion. The bird had thanked her before flying off.

Kelly flew over to Ary and scooped her up. "Nice work young fairy," he said as he carried her up. "You'll have wings in no time."
He could see that Ary was tired, though, so he said no more except: "Just point me towards your nest and I'll carry you home." Ary lifted a tired hand and with an extended finger, pointed the way home.

𝒮*tory no.* 4
Arylide's Third Act of Kindness

Arylide was a young wingless fairy who lived on a branch of the Great Tree at the edge of the Forest of Songs. These are the stories of her first year.

Image 9: Cerise

It was late Spring and there were many different varieties of flowers spread across the floor of the Forest of Songs. These flowers were different from those of the early Spring and there were so many colors and hues as well as wonderful odors that filled the air. The waterfall next to the Great Tree was roaring with a rush of water from the melting snow and the sun's rays were getting warmer with each day.

Ary was visiting with her friend the old yellow-winged fairy: Amber. She loved to visit with her friend on warm sunny afternoons because Ary could talk with her and answer her questions. On this day, Ary sat on the edge of Amber's nest and looked out across the forest. She saw birds flying high above that were twisting and soaring in the breezes. She saw squirrels jumping along the branches trying to find nuts before other fairies could grab them. She saw a rabbit peek its head out from a bush and then scamper off. She even saw a rare deer in the distance before it raised its tail and ran off into the deep woods.

Ary sat down on the feathers and twigs and crossed her hands in front of her. "There are so many creatures," she said in amazement. "There are creatures that fly and creatures that jump and creatures that crawl and climb."

"And there are many more creatures that you have not even seen yet." Amber added. "There are some that swim and some that walk on multiple legs and some that even live in the dirt."

"But why so many?" Ary asked.

"Because the essence of Earth Mother is so grand and so vast that no one creature can possibly display her immense beauty and splendor. Each different creature and the variations even among the same type of creature is but a small sample of what makes up Earth Mother and Sky Father."

"So many, but from the same source," said Ary humbly. She watched the animals and fairies play for a few moments. Then, she turned toward Amber. "Do all creatures know this, Amber?"

Amber was busily shuffling through some papers and got distracted. "Know what?"

"That they really are all from the same thing?"

"Such a big question for such a young fairy. The answer is yes. Some, like us, know it like a fact while others just feel it, but all creatures know it in some manner or another. All creatures except one, that is."

"One?"

"Yes, the humans."

"Humans? Do they live in the woods?" Ary asked.

"No, but they live all around us."

"What are they like?"

Amber put down her papers and sat down as if she knew this was going to be a long talk.

"They look like us only they are much bigger... and they don't have wings. No one knows if they came before us or if we came later but we definitely developed differently. They have come to believe that they are in control of nature rather than connected to it like all others," she said.

"How sad," Ary commented.

"What is truly sad is that they have caused great destruction and pain to Earth Mother and to other creatures. Fairies like us used to inhabit every stretch of woods in every land but their destruction of trees and land have limited where we can safely live in peace. There are not many of us left."

"Will they ever learn the truth?" Ary asked.

"We can only hope." Amber sighed.

Ary stretched out her arms and yawned. "Well," she sighed, "I think that I will do fine if I never meet one of those humans."

"All beings are worthy of respect," Amber reminded her. "Even humans."

"I suppose," Ary sighed as she yawned again. After a few moments, she said, "I think I will find some sweet sap to eat and then head back to my nest."

"I have food here, if you like."

"Oh, Amber," she began, "you're always so kind to me but it's such a warm evening that I think I would like to just move about the tree."

"As you wish," replied Amber as she reached for another book.

Image 10: An Owl

Arylide crawled out of the nest and started climbing down the tree. The Great Tree had plenty of sap to spare for the fairies. To find it they would put their noses next to the tree and smell a place where the sap was close to the surface. Then they would scratch gently at the surface until the sap flowed. The Tree would quickly heal afterwards and there were never too many fairies to cause stress to the Tree.

Ary moved along the trunk of the Great Tree and let her nose guide her. She could smell the sweet sap but continued to search until the sap smelled like it was very close. She moved to and fro while following the scent. Finally, she found a spot and gently peeled back just a tiny bit of the bark until some thick sweet liquid came up to the surface. Ary dipped her fingers into the sap and then licked them. It tasted so good but she only needed a small amount to fill her. As she was tasting the sap, she thought she heard a strange sound but it was so faint that she quickly ignored it. But then, it came again. It was a soft whimpering sound and it was coming from a nearby branch. Ary stopped eating and listened. There - she heard it again - a gentle crying sound. Ary licked the sap off of her fingers until they were clean and she gently replaced the bark on the tree so it could heal. Then, she kept listening and followed the sound until it brought her to a nest.

Ary found the nest from where the sound was coming and peeked over the edge. Suddenly, there came a flurry of activity. First, there were several varieties of birds that came flying out in all directions then other creatures like squirrels and mice and even insects came hurriedly out of the nest. There was even a grand old owl that flew out of the nest. Ary ducked while the different animals came flying over and around her. When they all had cleared away, Ary slowly and carefully looked into the nest. Inside was a female pink-winged fairy sitting on the floor and sobbing softly.

"You scared away my friends," the pink fairy sobbed.

"I'm sorry," replied Ary. "I heard you crying and wanted to see what was wrong. Should I go?"

"No. It's all right. I would like it if you stayed."

"I'm Arylide, Ary for short," said Ary.

"I'm Cerise," said the other fairy, drying her tears.

"Why are you sad, Cerise?" asked Ary.

"One of my friends, a rabbit, died a few days ago and I miss him so much."

"Is he not coming back?"Ary asked.

Cerise suddenly stopped sobbing and looked back at the young fairy. "You've not had someone or some other you know die have you?" said Cerise.

"No, I suppose not. " Ary felt embarrassed. Even though Cerise was not much older than Ary, (about a year) she had already grown her wings and had experienced many things by having so many creatures as friends. You see, Cerise loved everyone and everything even more deeply than most fairies.

"It's all right, Ary. It's not something any young fairy should experience but sometimes it does happen. It means my friend the rabbit is not coming back. I am not so sad for my friend as I am for myself. He will return to the arms of Earth Mother and be at peace but I shall miss him for a very long time. We used to play in the woods and run through the fields."

Ary just listened intently while Cerise continued. "One time," Cerise continued, "we were running in the field and a hawk spotted him. I heard it just in time to distract it while he ran to his rabbit hole. He would help me chase squirrels while I collected nuts. Oh..." Cerise got quiet for a moment and then started crying again. "I miss him so much," she sobbed.

Ary simply walked over to Cerise and put her arms around her - careful not to touch her delicate wings.

Cerise looked up at Ary and whispered a soft: "Thank you."

"For what?" asked Ary.

"For listening. That's all that I needed: someone who would just listen to me." After a few moments of crying Cerise quieted down. "Someday I will do the same for you."

Ary said nothing in response but just held her new friend tight as she cried herself to sleep.

𝒮tory no. 5
Arylide Learns To Fly

Arylide was a young winged fairy who lived on a branch of the Great Tree at the edge of the Forest of Songs. These are the stories of her first year.

Image 11: Arylide with Clear Wings

On this, the first day of Summer, Ary stood with her toes hanging over the edge of a high branch looking down to the ground that was a long way away from her. She was both excited and terrified at the same time.

"Well?" came a voice from behind her. It was her new friend Cerise, the pink-winged fairy.

"Give me a chance." Ary said with a shaky voice.

"Someone just pushed me my first time," said Cerise.

"Why haven't you just pushed me, then?"

"Because, although it worked, it was a cruel thing to do. I never want to do anything to any other creature that I wouldn't want done to me. But...if you are going to take all day I might have to push you."

"You wouldn't," murmured Ary.

"O.K., you're right. I wouldn't but it's the Summer Solstice and we have things to do, so jump already!"

"All right, all right," said Ary. She wasn't sure whether she should be more mad at Cerise or at herself.

It had only been a few weeks ago when Ary had woken up to a strange feeling in her back. It had been so itchy up until then but one day she woke up to find two lumps in her back. It became hard to sleep and she hoped they were something good and not something frightening. Her fears soon turned to hope when she noticed that the growth in her back started to develop into small appendages. Her dream had come true – she was finally growing her own wings.

During the next few weeks, her back would become a little painful and uncomfortable but Ary was willing to bear it all for the sake of her new wings. She would finally be a full fairy. Slowly the appendages grew and developed into two thin sheaths. The new wings kept growing and getting stronger until an even smaller set of lower wings developed as well. Finally, on this day of the Summer Solstice, the first day of Summer, Ary's wings were fully developed and she was ready to learn how to fly. Cerise was only a year older than her but had gone through this process already.

"Basically," Cerise had begun her instruction earlier that day, "All you have to do is jump and the wings will do the rest. They know what to do. Once you get going, you just concentrate on where you want to go. The wings simply follow your thoughts. It's really simple. It's just that first jump that's hard."

And that's where Ary was now – ready to take her first jump from a high branch off the Great Tree. She just needed the courage to do it.

"Ary!" cried Cerise bringing Arylide's mind back to the present. "Just do it!"

Ary looked out over the edge and steeped out just a little bit farther but she just couldn't jump. She thought back and tried to remember what she had done to deserve her wings. Amber, the great yellow-winged fairy, had told her that she needed to earn her wings by doing good deeds. What had she done? She remembered giving the hungry squirrels the nut she had tried to get for so long. She remembered helping Kelly, the green-winged fairy, fix a bird's wing, and she remembered taking the time to listen to Cerise when she was sad at losing her friend. Because she had done those things, Earth Mother had granted her wings and Sky Father had blessed them with strength. Now, she was ready to take her first jump...almost.

"Oh!" said Cerise in disgust. She got up and walked over to Ary.

"I thought you said you weren't going to push me," Ary said.

"I'm not," replied Cerise. She put her hand on Ary's quivering shoulder. "Look! I know how you feel but it will be all right. Flap your wings a little."

Ary did as her friend suggested and flapped her wings. The leaves around her waved as they were pushed by the rush of air coming from her wings.

"You see," said Cerise, "your wings are very strong and they will support you. Just remember to flap them as fast as possible until you feel them vibrate. Then you'll know that you are in control. If anything happens, I will fly down to you."

"Promise?" asked Ary.

"Promise!" replied Cerise as she patted Ary's shoulder. "You want to fly, right?"

"With all my heart," said Ary.

"Then focus on your desire and let it carry you," said Cerise as she went back to her seat.

Ary closed her eyes and thought about how wonderful it would be to finally fly like she saw all the other fairies fly. She just had to believe. She opened her eyes. Believe! She put her fears in check and shoved them aside. She felt only a desire to fly.

"Sky Father, catch me," she whispered to herself as she bent her knees and took a deep breath. Then...she jumped and all the world was silent.

Image 12: The Sunset

At first, Ary felt no fear as she glided downwards but then panic set in as her body started to twist and turn in mid-air. Her face and body smacked into leaves and twigs as she tumbled. She desperately tried to take control of her fear and concentrated on her wings. She continued to spin quickly towards the ground but she felt her wings start to move.

"Faster, faster!" she thought to herself. Her wings began to move more quickly and Ary could feel herself start to straighten out. "Even faster," she thought until she felt a strange vibration in her back. Then, she began to slow down. She concentrated harder and within just a few feet from the ground she suddenly stopped and just hovered.

"I did it! I really did it! I can fly!" She cried aloud and waved her arms. She heard the sound of Cerise as she flew beside her whooping and hollering.

"You did it!" Cerise called out.

Ary kept hollering and then suddenly stopped at looked at her friend. "Now what do I do?"

"Think where you want to go. Where your intention goes, you go."

Ary thought about going up. Within a moment she felt her wings change and she started to rise slowly.

"It works," she called out. Then, she tried moving in different directions: sideways, left, and right. She even tried zig-zagging. Within moments she was cheering and flying in all directions. Cerise soon joined her and they played by zipping in and around the branches of the Great Tree.

They played and dived and soared for a long time until they both landed on a branch and sat down together. They were both exhausted and just sat to enjoy the view.

It was late in the day and the sun was going down. As Ary sat watching, she noticed the other fairies getting more quiet as the sun got lower in the sky. As the sun began to reach the horizon, the others slowly flew up to the highest branches of the tree.

"What's going on?" Ary whispered.

"It's the Summer Solstice," Cerise softly replied. "It's the first day of Summer. Grandfather Sun will get weaker and weaker after tonight. The days will get shorter until Winter. It is both a sad and a joyous day for us. We celebrate the warmth of Summer but grieve the loss of light that starts tomorrow. On this night the fairies get quiet and observe the sunset from the highest branches. They also stay close to the trees because it is said that on this night the humans can see us if they look carefully so we try to stay hidden. Come on."

Cerise motioned to Ary to fly upwards and together they took off. Ary's flying was still unsteady but she managed to follow. At a branch very high up they landed and again sat down together. Around them were many of the fairies who were also sitting quietly and looking.

Together, they all watched as the sun began to fade beneath the horizon. Beautiful rays of crimson and gold played with soft puffy clouds as it descended. As the bright yellow sun disappeared, Ary heard a soft but lilting sound rise among the top branches of the tree. The fairies were singing gently and softly. It was a song filled both with sadness and gratitude. As Ary listened she learned the melody and gently joined in.

Suddenly, Ary felt a tug at her arm. Cerise was pointing into the woods. Ary strained her eyes to see in the darkening distance until she saw what had caught Cerise's attention. There at the edge of the woods was a young human boy who stood gazing into the trees. For just a brief moment, Ary thought the boy had seen her so she ducked but she could not be sure. Soon, however, the sun disappeared and darkness overtook the woods. The fairies quietly flew back to their own nests. In the small bit of light that the moon provided, Ary could see her friend Cerise give a friendly wink before she, too, flew off.

Ary sat for a few moments more holding the sights and sounds in her mind before she headed awkwardly towards her own nest. She took the opportunity to practice a few more loops and spins before going home.

Story no. 6
True Friendship

Arylide was a young wingless fairy who lived on a branch of the Great Tree at the edge of the Forest of Songs. These are the stories of her first year.

Image 13: The Waterfall and the Fairies

It was early Summer in the Forest of Songs and the days were getting hot and hazy. Arylide had spent the past few weeks perfecting her flying ability and was now pretty good at it. She decided to visit her friend Amber who had been teaching her things like how to read and write.

The old yellow-winged fairy, Amber, was sitting in her nest reading a book when she heard the buzz of wings that announced the approach of a fairy. She looked up to see Ary appear before her beaming with delight. Amber set down her book and stood up. "You got your wings! How wonderful!" she said as she opened her arms wide. Ary flew into her arms and accepted the hug.

"I am so happy for you," said Amber.

"Thank you," replied Ary. "I've been practicing every day. It feels so good to finally be flying."

"I'm glad to see that you are willing to stop flying long enough to continue your lessons, though."

"Well," said Ary, "I want to learn to read and write as well."

"I am glad to hear that. Shall we begin then?"

Amber reached up to find some books on a branch that she used as a shelf while Ary cleared a place to sit. As Amber came close to Ary with books in hand, Ary noticed the way her deep yellow wings looked so beautiful against the backdrop of the clear blue Summer sky.

"Amber?" asked Ary.

"Yes, dear," said Amber as she placed her books on a stone table.

Ary looked at herself, then said, "I don't seem to have a color on my wings."

"Not yet."

"Do I have to earn that too?"

"No. Your color is a reflection of who you are not what you do," said Amber as she opened up a book."

"And who am I?" asked Ary.

"Ah!" said Amber as she raised a wrinkled finger. "That's a big question."

"A big question?"

"Yes. You see there are big questions and there are little questions. If you were to ask people what color the sky was, nearly all of them would answer the same way."

"Blue!" called out Ary.

"Right," said Amber. "That's an example of a small question but a big question is one which everyone may have their own answer. Questions like 'who am I?' or 'why are we here?' are examples of big questions because each person you ask will probably give you a different answer. Big questions require that you seek out your own answer."

"So, if I want to find out who I am, I will need to find out for myself."

"That's right. You will need to explore; you will need to try new things until you find your own strengths and abilities. When you discover what it is that you are passionate about, you will discover your own color."

Ary put her head in her hands and thought about what Amber had said. She seemed disappointed to not get an easy answer to her question. But, after a few moments, she let it go and concentrated on the reason she was here.

"So, shall we?" she asked.

Amber took a look at Ary and saw how she was still struggling with the answer she had been given. She softly closed her book.

"I think you have enough to think about today," she said. "Why don't you take some time to go and play instead?"

Ary thought about it for a moment and then replied. "Well, O.K...see you later, then." And with those words, Ary spread her wings and flew out of Amber's nest and into the warm Summer air. She decided to look for her friend Cerise.

Image 14: Watching the Sunset

It didn't take to long to find Cerise. Ary practiced her fast flying and diving skills so that she could quickly check the main branches and play places around the Great Tree. She found her at the waterfall playing hide and seek in and around the water and rocks. Cerise was with two other young fairies: one was a very light green-winged female fairy while the other was a male fairy with a pale reddish wing color. They all seemed to be enjoying themselves. They laughed and shrieked as they flew close to the spray of the waterfall. Cerise saw Ary approaching and she waved.

Cerise flew down to a rock by the water and waited for Ary to join her.

"Hey, Ary!" called Cerise, still waving.

Ary landed beside her friend. "Hi, Cerise. What are you doing?"

"Just playing about in the water. I thought you had a lesson."

"Amber told me to take the day and play."

"Oh great," clapped Cerise.

Just then the other two fairies that had been playing with her landed nearby.

"Hey, Cerise," said the boy. "Are you coming?"

"Yea, sure," said Cerise. She pointed toward Ary. "This is my friend Ary." The two other fairies barely paid attention to Ary.

"C'mon, Cerise. Let's go play," said the girl.

"Yea, O.K. But I think Ary might want to join...."

"She can't play with us!" interrupted the boy.

"But, why not?" asked a bewildered Cerise.

"Cerise," said the girl with disgust in her voice. "Look at her. Her wings have no color."

"So what?" shot back Cerise. "We all had colorless wings once. She just hasn't found her color yet. Besides, what difference does color make?"

"All the difference in the world," said the boy and, with that, the two young fairies flew up into the air.

"C'mon," said the girl motioning to Cerise with her arm.

Cerise looked at the two other fairies and then looked to Ary. Ary looked at her friend and said, "It's O.K., Cerise. You can go and play with them. I don't mind."

"You don't?" Cerise looked surprised.

"You were having fun with them. Go on."

Cerise looked at Ary and then at her two friends who were still hovering above. "Go on without me," she called out to the two fairies. "I'm going to stay here." The two young fairies in the air both looked at each other and with sounds of disgust flew off.

"Why didn't you go with your friends?" asked Ary.

"They're not really very good friends if they reject one of my other friends just because of the way she looks. True friends love you for just being you. They have no need to persuade you to do things you don't want to do. Any friend who says that they can only like you as long as you do only what they want is not really a true friend after all. A true friend is one who says 'go on and play with them. I just want you to be happy.' A true friend is someone like you." Cerise looked at her friend. Ary returned the look and then hugged her.

Cerise started to cry. "But I was just starting to like them," she sobbed.

Ary gently rubbed her friends shoulders and whispered into her ear. "Oh, Cerise. You love everyone and everything."

"It's true," cried Cerise until the sound of her sobs were drowned out by the roar of the waterfall.

𝒮tory no. 7
Arylide Meets Scarlet

Arylide was a young winged fairy who lived on a branch of the Great Tree at the edge of the Forest of Songs. These are the stories of her first year.

Image 15: Scarlet

It was the height of Summer. The days were hot and the nights were warm as well. The fairies spent the warm days staying in their nests in the shade or they swam in the waters by the waterfall. On this day, Arylide decided she would find her friend Cerise. So, she took to the sky and flew towards Cerise's nest on the other side of the Great Tree. Though she flew in as quietly and softly as she could she, nonetheless, frightened off a whole collection of animals that always seemed to be hanging around her nest.

"Oh, Cerise, I'm sorry," said Ary as she landed in Cerise's nest. "I always seem to scare off all your friends when I come to visit."

"Well," replied the pink-winged fairy Cerise. "at least I can always know when you're coming."

"Why do all those creatures stay around your nest all the time, anyway?"

"Because I love them all so much and they love me in return."

Ary thought about this for a moment and then said. "Sounds wonderful. I'm really sorry I can't share that feeling with your friends when I come here."

"Maybe you can," said Cerise.

"What do you mean?"

"Well, all you need to do is open up your heart and let them experience the love that comes from within. That's what I do, anyway. Sometimes I can feel them call out to me. All fairies can experience what other beings are feeling but I like to send my message of love as well as receive it and the creatures seem to respond. Why not try it?"

Ary gave it some thought and then said, "So all I have to do is concentrate on sending out feelings of love and they will come?"

"No," replied Cerise. "Not exactly. You have to start with yourself. You have to be completely comfortable with who you are and what you are. You have to start with feelings of love toward yourself and then extend that feeling to all other beings. If you can't love yourself, then you can't fully love others. The animals that come here are attracted to the feelings of love I offer first to myself."

"That doesn't sound so hard," said Ary.

"For some it is very difficult."

Ary took some deep breaths and closed her eyes. She concentrated on her own feelings. She felt love and acceptance toward her own self. She loved being a fairy and enjoyed living in the Forest of Songs. She then focused on sending that feeling outward from herself in all directions. At first, it was hard to quiet her mind but she persisted until she had only feelings within her - feelings of joy and love. After several minutes she began to feel strange things. At first these feelings frightened her but she managed to calm herself and continue. When those feelings came back, she figured out that they were the other creatures who had just disappeared. They had not gone far and Ary began to feel the presence of each one. She embraced those feelings in her mind and thought about loving each of them as much as she loved herself. Slowly and cautiously the creatures began to return to the nest. Though she did not open her eyes, Ary knew they were there. When several had returned, she opened her eyes and saw a robin, a squirrel, and a long slender green snake. They looked still a little unsure about her but Ary moved slowly and kept sending feelings of love toward them.

"You learn quick," Cerise whispered to her friend. "Maybe next time you come they won't all run away."

"I hope you're right but that's not really why I came to see you."

"You know," said Cerise, "You don't need a reason to come see me."

"Oh yes I know that but I also know that another seasonal celebration is coming soon and I thought you might tell me what it is so I can actually know ahead of time for once."

"You're right. Tomorrow is a Cross-Quarter day when we celebrate the middle of Summer and the bounty of food that is available at this time. It is traditional to make things to decorate our nests and to share at the feast. Before the great feast we collect food from around the woods to share together."

"What kind of things do we make?" asked Ary."

"Whatever you want, really," replied Cerise. "I have an idea," she continued. "We could go visit my friend Scarlet. She loves to make all kinds of things."

Image 16: Art Work

"All right," agreed Ary and together the two fairies flew off with Cerise in the lead leaving their animal friends behind. Within just a few moments, Cerise had led Ary to a very colorful nest. Cerise and Ary both landed on the edge of the nest and peered in. Ary stood in amazement over what she saw. The oddly shaped nest was filled with all kinds of beautiful art work. There were paintings with many colors and shapes. There were objects made of clay and stone. There were musical instruments stored on various shelves that shared space with carvings, sculptures, and models. There were feather pens and sheets of brightly colored paper and there all kinds of strange objects, knick-knacks, and decorations.

Ary heard a noise and saw movement in a far corner. A red-winged fairy was busy gluing together flower petals and leaves into the shape of a large bowl.

"Um, excuse us," Cerise said gently.

"Huh?" The red fairy looked around to see who was there and noticed Ary and Cerise admiring her art work.

"Oh, hey! Blessed Season!" she beamed when she recognized Cerise. "Come on in!"

As they stepped in, Cerise motioned towards Ary. "Scarlet, this is my good friend Ary."

"Oh, hi Ary," said Scarlet.

Ary looked all around her at all the wonderful things that Scarlet made. "Everything is so beautiful. Did you make all these things?"

"Yes," replied Scarlet.

Cerise stepped in closer. We were hoping you might help us make something for the feast tomorrow night."

"Oh sure," said Scarlet. "Use anything you like."

"Thanks Scarlet," said Cerise as she grabbed a feather pen and some paper. Soon Cerise was drawing what she saw when she looked out at the Forest of Songs. "C'mon," she said to Ary. Ary came over to see what Cerise was doing.

She looked at her drawing and saw that it wasn't as precise as the drawings that Scarlet had strewn around her nest but it was still nice to see. Ary picked up another pen and some paper and tried her hand at drawing, but every time she tried to draw something, it just turned out to look like a mess.

"Oh!" cried out Ary in frustration. "I can't do this!"

Scarlet stopped what she was doing and walked over to Ary to see what she was doing.

"Have you ever drawn before?" she asked.

"No."

"Well, you have to give yourself a chance. Some people spend a lifetime learning how to draw."

"But I can't even seem to draw a simple circle or cloud or anything."

"Well, you don't always have to draw common objects. Sometimes it's fine to just draw lines or abstract shapes."

"But I just can't seem to even do that."

"It may be that drawing is not your strength but there are so many other ways to create. You just have to explore and discover what you feel you can do. You could try painting, or making things, or creating music, or dancing, or any number of creative things."

"Hmm, dancing," Ary hummed. Then, she started moving her body. At first, her movements were just little motions made with her hands and fingers Then, she started moving her arms and her shoulders. She added movements with her feet and within moments she was moving her whole body in beautiful arcs and curves. After seeing what Ary was doing, Scarlet grabbed a flute that was hanging on a branch and started playing a soft lilting tune that seemed to go so well with Ary's movements. As if on cue, Cerise found a small drum and added some rhythm to the music.

The three fairies danced and laughed and played until they all fell together exhausted.

The next night, Ary, Cerise, and Scarlet got together and took their art works and instruments to one of the largest branches on the Great Tree. Fairies from all over the tree gathered together at the branch and spread out food that they all had collected. There were dozens of dishes made from nuts and berries, nectar, honey, grains, mushrooms, and anything else that could be found in the Forest of Songs. All the fairies feasted, talked, and sang songs. Some offered their art works for others to view and Ary danced while Cerise and Scarlet played. The celebration went long into the warm evening.

Story no. 8
Amber Returns to Earth Mother

Arylide was a young winged fairy who lived on a branch of the Great Tree at the edge of the Forest of Songs. These are the stories of her first year.

Image 17: Moonlight

It was late Summer and the days were very hot. Many of the fairies spent their afternoons staying cool in the shade or playing in the water of the great waterfall and creek. Late Summer was also the time human children were off from school and, sometimes, spent their time playing in the Great Woods. The fairies that stayed up in the tree simply hid from the children behind leaves and branches. Other fairies, especially the younger fairies, enjoyed playing games and tricks with the human children. Sometimes objects the kids were playing with would disappear or would show up in another place. Sometimes the fairies would drop objects in the woods hoping the sound might scare the children. At other times, some brave fairies even let themselves be seen by a single child for a brief time so that the other humans would laugh at him or her for claiming to see little winged people.

Fairies, like Cerise and Scarlet, often joined in these games just for fun but Ary found that she did not enjoy that activity as much as she did just reading and learning about things. The yellow-winged fairy Amber had taught her to read and write and now Ary had a great interest in books and ideas. She would often borrow books from Amber's vast library or she would find out about other books and manuscripts written by other fairies.

On this warm day, Ary was doing her favorite thing - reading a book. She had built up the walls around her nest with thick green leaves and had done the same to the space above it as well. The leaves kept out the heat of the sun. She opened spaces among the leaves so that the breezes that wafted through the branches could come in and keep her cool. If it got too hot in the middle of the day, she would dive down to the creek and splash in the water for a bit before returning to her books.

As Ary sat reading, she heard a rush of wings approach her nest. It was a red-winged fairy, her friend Scarlet, who hovered where Ary could see her through one of the vents.

"Ary!" cried out Scarlet. "Don't you ever stop reading?"

"It's a good book and, besides, I've only been reading for a short time," Ary responded.

"You've been reading all morning!"

"All morning?" said Ary in surprise. "Is it afternoon already?" She looked up and noticed that the sun had passed the midpoint of the sky.

"Oh my, I suppose it is!" she said.

Scarlet landed in Ary's nest and folded her wings. "Why don't you take a break and come down to the forest with some of us? We thought we might collect some berries for dinner."

Ary thought about it for a moment. "I suppose I could use a break."

She put her book down and stood up. Scarlet took off first and Ary followed. For a while they played follow-the-leader as Ary carefully imitated everything Scarlet did. The red-winged fairy was taking great delight in swooshing between branches. She did flips and rolls in the air. Sometimes she would make a quick dive straight down or she would rise upwards in a spiral pattern. At other times she flew in a straight line as fast as she could and then she would, all of a sudden, fly backwards. Ary was confident in her flying abilities now and was proud that she could keep up with Scarlet every step of the way.

After quite a while of doing these flying acrobatics, Ary and Scarlet landed together on a rock near the creek.

"You're pretty good for a newbie flyer," Scarlet laughed.

"Thanks for the practice," responded Ary.

They both sat for a moment to catch their breath when Scarlet jumped into the air pointing toward the deep woods. "I think there are some juicy blackberry bushes over in that direction."

Ary jumped up into the air as well. "Let's go then," she said.

As they were flying off, Scarlet turned to Ary and said: "See if you can find a nice green leaf on the ground so that you can carry your berries back."

Each of them dove down to the forest floor and picked up a soft leaf and then continued on their way to the berry bush. Scarlet hovered above a thick bush and waited for Ary to catch up.

"O.K.," she said. "This is it. But, be careful. There are some thorns in the bushes."

Ary nodded and they both descended carefully at the edge of the bush. There they found plenty of full ripe berries and they each began collecting an arm load. As they searched, the two slowly drifted apart. It wasn't long before Ary found herself alone in the berry patch. She didn't seem too concerned, however, because there were still a lot of juicy berries surrounding her. She noticed one particularly plump berry that was under a fallen branch and she started to head toward it when she heard a distant voice.

"Ary! Stop!" called Scarlet from high above her. "Don't move!"

Ary stopped what she was doing and turned around to see Scarlet racing toward her as fast as she could. Scarlet landed next to Ary.

"What is it?" asked Ary.

"Look over there." Scarlet was pointing toward the berry that Ary had seen and was about to go after.

"I don't see anything," said Ary but Scarlet was still pointing.

"Look closer!" demanded Scarlet.

Ary looked and looked but saw nothing other than the ripe berry. Then, she tilted her head a bit and saw a glimmer of light. There WAS something there! Ary kept moving and tilting her head until, suddenly, the light of the sun revealed directly in front of her the intricate pattern of a large spider web.

"Oh, my goodness," she gasped.

Scarlet turned towards her. A little further and you might have gotten tangled in that sticky web and hiding somewhere nearby is its owner."

"The spider?" Ary asked. "Would it have hurt me?"

"It may have nipped you, paralyzed you, and spun you into a big ball just to teach you a lesson but you don't have anything it wants."

"Thank you for stopping me, then. I think we ought to just leave it alone. I have plenty of berries already."

"Wise choice. Let's go," said Scarlet and the two carefully rose up into the air holding their berries and made their way back to Scarlet's nest. After they landed and set down their berries on a stone table, Ary turned towad Scarlet.

"Thanks for stopping me from running into that web, Scarlet," she said.

"Sure thing, Ary," replied Scarlet but even before she could finish her thought, they both saw Cerise heading quickly toward them. They knew right away that something was wrong. Cerise stopped suddenly in front of them.

"Ary! Come quick! It's Amber!" she gasped. The three fairies rushed off to Amber's nest as fast as they could go.

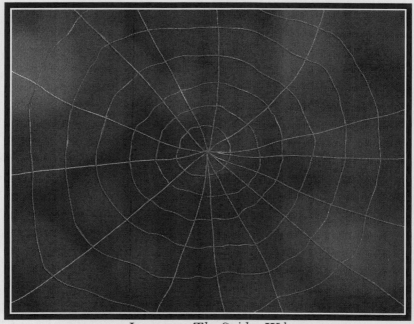

Image 18: The Spider Web

When they got to the old fairy's nest, Ari saw her old yellow-winged friend sitting in her chair made of acorns. She looked tired and frail. Ari flew over to her and kneeled by her side taking her hand.

"Amber," she whispered.

Amber put her other hand over Ari's hand. "Oh, Ari. I think I shall miss you most of all."

"Amber, where are you going?"

"It's my time. I have been in this realm for many years but now I must return to Earth Mother and Sky Father so that new life may be born."

"I don't understand," Ari whimpered.

Cerise walked up to Ari, put her hand on her friend's shoulder, and whispered: "She's dying, Ari."

Ari began crying and put her forehead on Amber's arm. The yellow-winged fairy rose up slowly from her seat. She took Ari and cradled her head against her chest and held her tight and let her cry for several moments. Then, she lifted Ari's chin towards her and looked into her eyes.

"I want you to take care of my things for me. They are all yours now," said Amber.

She helped Ary, who was still crying, to get to her feet and she hugged her for a long time. Then, she walked to the edge of her nest. Amber spread her wings out full but did not fly.

She turned her head and said to all the fairies standing there: "Be kind. Be considerate. Be true." She then jumped into the air. All three fairies ran to the edge of the nest and saw Amber glide downwards. There was a small glimmer of light that rose upwards from her body as she drifted and then her body became still and stiff. It began to resemble a dry leaf and drifted to and fro in the warm breeze as any leaf that fell from the Great Tree might do until it landed softly on the ground. There, it blended in with the dirt, wood, and grass until it was gone.

That night, after Cerise and Scarlet had left, Ari stayed on in Amber's nest and cried herself to sleep.

𝒮tory no. 9
The Storm

Arylide was a young winged fairy who lived on a branch of the Great Tree at the edge of the Forest of Songs. These are the stories of her first year.

Image 19: Storm Cloud

𝒾t was the Autumn equinox and the beginning of Fall. In the Forest of Songs the days were becoming very warm but the nights were quite cool. The nights gave the first hint that the colder months were on their way. Some of the leaves on the trees of the Great Woods were already beginning to change colors. Light hints of yellow, crimson, and orange were sprinkled throughout the woods.

Ary was napping in the late afternoon as did many fairies in the late Summer when she was awoken by the sound of distant thunder. Though it was obviously far off, the sound had been strong enough to wake her. She rose slightly and looked around. In the weeks after her friend Amber had returned to Earth Mother, Ary had stayed in her friend's nest. Amber had entrusted her with all of her books and belongings and Ary took her charge seriously. She had decided to stay in Amber's nest and give her old one to another young fairy who needed one. She was thankful for the chance to read some of the many books and pamphlets that filled the nest. She knew it would be a long time before she would be able to get through all of them but she enjoyed reading and learning new things and knew she would enjoy the challenge of trying to read them all.

Another loud boom rocked the trees. Ary decided to fly to the top of the tree and see what might be coming. Just above the highest branch of the Great Tree were several fairies looking to the West with a concerned look on their faces. She looked in the direction from which they were pointing and saw a large, dark, and menacing cloud in the distance. They all knew there was a powerful storm coming their way.

Ary quickly flew down to find her friends. She first found Cerise. Usually, when Ary came to Cerise's nest, there were all kinds of animals visiting - but not today.

"Where are all your animal friends?" asked Ary as she landed in Cerise's nest. Cerise was busy building up walls with extra branches, paper, dirt, and anything else she could find.

"They knew there was a terrible storm coming long before the first thunderclap," Cerise replied. As she talked the sky grew very dark. Ary looked around at what Cerise had been doing.

"You're going to need some help, I think," said Ary.

"But, what about your nest?" asked Cerise.

"We'll work faster if we do it together. We can get yours fixed up and then work on mine."

"O.K.," agreed Cerise and they started working together. As they worked to build some solid walls, they heard Scarlet approach. She landed in the nest.

"Can you two help me with my nest? I think we're in for a big one," she asked.

"Sure, Scarlet," said Ary. "We just need to finish up here first."

"I can help," said Scarlet as she grabbed some leaves. As she started working, rain began to fall in on them. It started first as a thin mist and turned quickly into a light rain but, before long, it became a great torrent of water that fell upon the three fairies with a powerful force.

"You're going to need a strong roof," Ary called out against the sound of the pouring rain. The three fairies collected more twigs, branches, and leaves and built a roof over the nest. As they worked, the wind began to pick up as well as the rain. They struggled to work against the forces of the storm. As they pulled and pushed and fought the wind and rain, they managed to get a small roof up. The wind continued to get stronger and thunder and lightning ripped through the woods.

At one point, one of the twigs they had placed on the side of the nest managed to work its way loose. Cerise managed to grab it but then lost her balance as a gust of wind pulled her off the nest.

"Cerise!" Ary yelled as she went over to her and grabbed her hand. Cerise's wings were just not strong enough to resist the strength of the storm's winds. The storm threatened to carry her off and away but Ary held on tight to her hand. The only problem was that Ary was having a hard time finding something to hang on to so she could anchor herself and pull in Cerise.

"Scarlet!" Ary called out. Scarlet had not heard Cerise's cries over the sound of the wind and thunder but when she heard Ary call out, she dropped what she was doing and ran to her. She grabbed Ary around her waist and held on tight. Ary felt Scarlet's arms around her and was glad to be firmly held in the nest but she was slowly losing grip on Cerise's hand.

"I can't hold on!" cried Cerise. Ary tried as hard as she could to keep her hand locked with her friend's hand but she knew it was only a matter of time.

"Cerise! Hold on!" Ary cried out in vain. She could feel Cerise's fingers slipping out of her own. Just when she was about to lose her friend to the whims of the wind she heard a faint sound and saw something approach behind Cerise. It was Kelly, the green-winged fairy. He caught Cerise just as she was about to be carried off. Somehow, he was just strong enough to fight the wind and put Cerise down in the nest but it was easy to see that he had used almost all his strength to do it. Cerise thanked him but there was little time to talk. With Kelly's help, the fairies were able to finish fortifying Cerise's nest against the storm. Even though they were all exhausted, Ary went to the edge of the nest and looked out.

"I've got to save my nest!" Ary whimpered.

Image 20: The Feast

The other fairies looked at her and knew what she was thinking. They didn't have to say the obvious, though. There was no way that any of them were going to be able to leave this nest until the storm was over. They just had to hope for the best. Cerise walked over to Ary and put her arms around her. Together, they walked back to the center of the nest to wait. Just beyond the newly built walls of the nest, the storm raged on. They all huddled together and fell asleep from exhaustion.

The next morning, the four fairies woke to bright sunshine and the sound of birds singing. Cerise's animal friends had returned but kept some distance due to the new faces in the nest. As they rose, the fairies began to clear out the debris and mess caused by the storm. While Kelly and Cerise continued to clean up, Ary turned to Scarlet.

"C'mon," she said to the red-winged fairy. "Let's go see how your home weathered the storm." The two took off into the sunny morning and headed toward Scarlet's nest. When they got there, they both hovered nearby and stared in disbelief. The place was in shambles. Art work, instruments, music, pieces of sculpture, and various creations lay strewn all over and around a jumble of leaves, twigs, mud, and other debris. Scarlet landed on the edge of her nest and started to cry. Fearing the worst, Ary flew off to her own nest. When she arrived, her heart sunk. The nest was in a great wreck as well. Books, papers, and pamphlets were torn and damaged all over the nest. Instead of crying, she decided to return to Cerise's nest until she could get over the feelings of pain and loss. She knew she would not be able to start cleaning up just yet.

Ary arrived back at Cerise's nest and sat down feeling depressed. Kelly had flown off to clean up his own area and Cerise knew by the look on Ary's face what she had found. Cerise just put her arm around her and whispered, "I'm sorry." Scarlet also returned and, together, the three of them sat in silence.

After several moments of heavy sorrow, Scarlet broke the silence. "Not much to be thankful about, is there?"

"Scarlet, what are you talking about?" asked Cerise.

"Yesterday," Scarlet responded.

"Yesterday? What was yesterday?" asked Ary.

"The Fall Equinox," whispered Cerise recalling the seasonal celebration.

"Fall Equinox," repeated Ary to herself. She began thinking back on some of the books she had read that explained the sacred days and their meanings. "the Fall Equinox is when we give thanks for what we have and consider what we have done with our lives over the past year."

Cerise spoke next. "We often get together and count our blessings for what we have."

"I've lost my art. I have nothing," bemoaned Scarlet.

"And I've lost all my books," added Ary.

Cerise looked at her friends and said: "And the two who are most important to me have lost their happiness."

The silence lasted for what seemed an eternity but then was broken by Ary.

"No, wait," she said. This isn't right. I may have lost books and, Scarlet, you may have lost valuable works of beauty, but we still have each other. We still have things for which we can be thankful. I think we should celebrate the Fall Equinox after all."

Scarlet stopped crying and dried her tears. "You're right, Ary," she said. "Those works are still in my heart and I can bring them back but we still are friends and we still have each other."

"And I can collect books again," remarked Ary.

"Come, then," said Cerise as she cleared off a table and put together some seats for them to sit on. She went into a small trunk tucked away in the back of the nest.

"I've been saving this," she said as she pulled out a special loaf of bread, some cheese, and the traditional berry drink for this seasonal celebration. She put them on the table and poured drinks for her friends.

The three gathered at the table and took the cups but did not drink. Cerise took the bread and broke off a piece for each of them. She said: "I break bread with you to share my love for each of you." They each took a bite. Then, one at a time, each of them raised their glass and mentioned the things that they were thankful for. When they had all spoken, they drank together.

"Blessed Season!" they said together.

𝒮tory no. 10
Arylide Meets Han

Arylide was a young yellow-winged fairy who lived on a branch of the Great Tree at the edge of the Forest of Songs. These are the stories of her first year.

Image 21: Han

It was early autumn in the Forest of Songs. This was the time of the year when the leaves of the trees began to show their brightest and deepest colors. The woods were filled with leaves of fire red, pumpkin orange, and sun-drenched yellow. Though the nights were starting to get cool, the days were still warm and the fairies could not help but stare in awe at the sight around them. It helped to lift their spirits.

For weeks, many of them had been cleaning up from the devastating late Summer storm that had hit the Forest just a few weeks ago. Many of the fairy nests had been damaged or destroyed by the wind and the water. Those few fairies with little damage to their homes spent time helping out the others make repairs and rebuild. By now, however, most of the nests were near completion and the fairies could start to slow down and enjoy thhe beauty that now surrounded them.

The young fairy Ary had been one of those who had needed to rebuild. Not only was the nest she had been living in mostly ruined, so were the many books and papers that she had stored. Her friend Scarlet, the artist, also had great damage done to her nest. Their friend Cerise was able to help them whenever she could.

On this warm and sunny day, Ary was in her nest finishing some cleaning and clearing out of the last bits of debris left over from the storm. Her friend Cerise was helping the red-winged fairy Scarlet finish up her nest. Ary discarded the last bit of sticks and mud that had caked her nest floor for so long and then washed up with a bowl of water from the creek below. She stood back and looked over the whole scene. Though the place was now clean, it was not back to its original condition. There were many empty shelves and branches where books and other ideas had been stored for so long. Ary was filled with feelings of sadness and anger.

The shelves were not completely empty, however. All the fairies were committed to helping each other out and when some had heard about what had happened to her books, they brought her any extra copies they had to help her fill her shelves. Her old friend, Amber, who had given her this nest and all its books, had been collecting works for a long time and there were still plenty of empty spaces.

Ary wiped her hands and stood back to look at the place. As she stood in both admiration for all the work done and frustration at the still obvious loss, she heard the sound of wings behind her. Thinking it might be one of her friends, Ary wheeled around quickly with a smile but stopped short when she saw something unexpected. Standing before her was a rather large male purple-winged fairy. In his arms were several large books. He floated there for several moments observing the scene. Then, he turned to Ary.

"Are you Arylide?" he asked.

"Most call me Ary," she replied.

"Well, then, Ary," he said. "May I enter? I brought you some books." He looked about. "I understand you need some."

"Yes. Yes I do," she said.

The purple-winged fairy came into the nest and landed near one of the empty spaces reserved for books.

"May I?" he asked pointing to the shelf.

"Sure," she answered him.

He put the large books onto the shelf and then turned back to her. "My name is Han," he said.

"Thank you, Han," she said as she walked over to the shelf and looked over the spines of the new books. She read some of the titles out loud. They were : "The Movements of Celestial Bodies," "The Collected Works of Carmine," and "Attuning With the Natural Elements." She turned towards the purple-winged fairy.

"Thank you, Han," she said.

Han turned to fly away but heard Ary whimpering lightly. She was exhausted, frustrated, and angry. Han turned about and put his arms around her. Ary cried for a moment and then pulled away in anger.

"Oh why did that storm have to destroy everything?" she cried out.

"I don't want to sound insensitive because I know that you are in pain over your loss but there is good that can come from this," said Han.

"What do you mean?" asked Ary.

"You see," began Han motioning for them to sit down, "destruction is not an ending but part of the endless cycle of change. Nature knows no straight lines or endings. With each end comes the chance for renewal. The storm makes it possible to begin anew."

Ary looked at him with anger and confusion. "Do you mean the purpose of that storm was to destroy things so that new things can take their place?"

"No, not at all," replied Han. "The purpose of the storm is only to be a storm but all things are in and part of the process of being and becoming."

"That doesn't make the loss any less painful," she shot back.

"No, of course not," he agreed. "But it can help us to find ways to seek meaning and hope for the future." Han looked closer into Ary's eyes.

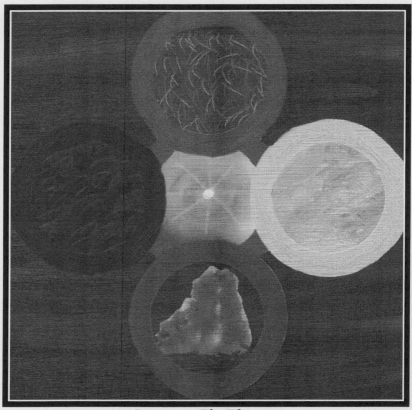

Image 22: The Elements

"You have a gift," he said. "You enjoy learning and you like to write."

"But how do you know that?" Ary asked in amazement because she knew he was right.

"Your wings," he responded. "They are a light yellow color."

"They are?"

It was very difficult for fairies to see their own wings unless they looked at a reflection from the still waters of the pool below the waterfall. She noticed before that her wings, when they finally grew, had no color. She had taken care to notice their clear and beautiful shape when she had gone swimming at the creek but they must have been changing in the last few weeks. All the fairies had been so busy cleaning up from the storm that no one had noticed or remarked about the change of color - until now, that is.

Han continued. "Yellow is the color of the element of Air and Air represents the mental part of ourselves. The fact that your wings are slightly yellow means that you favor using your mind over the other parts of yourself. You probably enjoy reading and communicating to others - especially through writing."

"Yes it's true," said Ary. She had spent many hours trying to reconstruct some of the damaged books by writing what she thought might be missing. She realized how much she enjoyed the act of writing.

"The elements!" Ary murmured. "That's the subject of one of the books you just gave me," she said to the other fairy.

"Yes, that's right," he responded. "The elements help to represent what I've been talking about. They represent states of change."

"What are these elements?"

"Earth, Air, Fire, and Water," said Han. "Each of them make a part of the whole."

Ary looked perplexed so Han took another breath and tried again.

"Let's take real water as an example. In the Summer, water exists in a liquid state. When fire is applied to it, such as through the heat of the summer sun, the water evaporates and becomes part of the air. As it collects together, it comes back to the earth as rain. In the Winter, the water becomes more solid as it turns into snow and ice. Though the water can take many forms it is, in reality, all one thing. The same is true with us. Though we are each one fairy, we have mental, emotional, physical, and spiritual parts. In your case, you can transform the old and lost books that you once had into new works. You can restore old writing and you can write new books based on new ideas."

"But I don't know how!" Ary exclaimed.

"Writing intensely does involve some important skills like research, creating an outline, disciplining yourself to write, and it involves being open to ideas. I can teach you many of those things if you'd like."

Ary did not really have to think about it for very long. The idea of creating new books was exciting to her.

"I would like that," she said.

"Great, I will come back tomorrow after breakfast and we will begin," he said and he started to head out but Ary stopped him.

"Han?" she said.

"Yes?" He said turning back around.

"What is your passion?"

Han chuckled. "Teaching!" and then flew off into the warm air.

Ary smiled as she watched him go.

Story no. 11
Arylide Learns Meditation from Old Azure

Arylide was a young yellow-winged fairy who lived on a branch of the Great Tree at the edge of the Forest of Songs. These are the stories of her first year.

Image 23: Old Azure

It was the height of Autumn and the past few weeks had been a blaze of color throughout the Great Woods. The tremendous storm that had ripped through the woods soaked the trees but in the days afterward the air had been mostly warm and dry while the evenings were crisp and cool. It was the perfect condition for a dazzling display from Earth Mother. The reds, yellows, oranges, and browns filled the fairies hearts with joy and awe. By now, nearly all the nests had been rebuilt and the debris from the storm had been cleared out.

As she had been doing for several weeks now, Ary and the purple-winged fairy, Han, were sitting at a stone table together. Ary had come far in learning how to do research and write important books. They had been working together through most of the day and now, the sun was beginning to set and a clear dark sky was coming into focus overhead Soon, the stars would pierce through the coming darkness. At one point, Ary closed the book she had been reading and looked up at Han.

"That's it. I don't think I can do anymore today," she said with a heavy sigh.

Han closed a book as well and leaned back. "It's o.k. You've done enough for today. Besides, it's a sacred day and you deserve a break. You're almost done with the lessons anyway. Soon you will be finished."

"Another sacred day," she murmured to herself. "Let me see. It must be the height of Autumn."

"That's right," said Han. "It's the Autumn Cross-quarter and a very sacred night. Earth Mother retreats into the darkness of Winter and we honor that darkness. Through the stars of the night we also honor our ancestors.

For many of us it is also a good time for meditation and divination."

Ary looked at him with a blank stare.

"Ah, yes, of course," said Han. "You have not had much experience with those things."

"What makes you say that?" asked Ary.

"Your wings, again," replied Han. "They say a lot about you. Fairies with dark colored wings have experienced the connection."

"The connection?"

"The connection between all things," said Han.

"Can you teach me how to experience that connection?"

"I can only teach you what I know. There is yet another fairy who can teach you much better than I. Are you sure you really want to do this, though? It is not easy work and, I must warn you, Azure is not the easiest fairy to work with so you need to be sure."

"I would like to give it a try at least."

"Very well, then, come with me," said Han and the two fairies flew off into the fading light of the dusk. Ary followed Han through the branches. She expected to be taken to yet another nest on the Great Tree but Han kept flying downward until they were just above the ground. Then, Han banked hard and flew along the side of the creek that lead away from the waterfall. Finally, he stopped by a large rock that covered a mound of dirt. Ary followed him into a dark cave lit by small candles inside.

"Hello?" called out Han into the cave. When there came no response, he called again. He moved further into the dark and called yet again. "Hello? Are you in?" Ary went into the cave behind Han.

Still, the two were greeted only by silence but Ary felt the presence of something from within. Han shrugged his shoulders then turned around to leave but before he could reach the entrance of the cave, there was a faint sound. Han stopped in his tracks and turned his head to give a mysterious smile to Ary. He turned his head back around.

"So you are here! Blessed Season!" he bubbled, but there was still only silence. Han waited. After a long quiet moment, there was a sound and the face of an old fairy appeared out of the shadows.

"Go away, Han!" it sputtered.

"Azure, you're looking ravishing as usual," teased Han but the face did not laugh. In fact, it barely moved. Ary couldn't help but feel something strange.

"Go off with you. I'm busy."

"Azure, in all the years I've known you, you have always worked hard at not being busy."

More of the face came out of the shadows until the front half of an elderly fairy appeared before them.

"Exactly, my dear friend," said Azure. "That is why you'll understand it when I tell you to go away."

Han turned toward the face in the corner. "Ah, but then, my dear and wise friend, if we go you won't have the chance to meet this wonderful young fairy." Han pointed towards Ary who was staring from near the front entrance. The face moved slowly and looked in the direction of the visitor. She gave the young fairy a look-over and then turned back towards Han. The strange feeling that was inside Ary was growing stronger.

"She looks like any other young foolish fairy out there. Why should I waste my time with this impetuous thing?"

Ary felt awful being in the presence of this strange creature. She wanted to fly right out of there but Han continued to talk to her.

"She wants to learn about meditation," Han said confidently.

Han had said something that made the old fairy be silent for a moment. Then, she walked out of the shadows. Ary expected her to move erratically and in fits and starts but that wasn't what happened. Instead, the elderly fairy moved gracefully and with beautiful motions like a swan moving across still water. When she had flowed out of the shadows, Ary saw the most amazing and beautiful pair of wings she had ever seen. They were blue but not just one shade of blue; there were many shades of blue on them and each went from lighter to darker hues. Each shade of blue was intense but the combination of all of them together made the wings all that more impressive. Ary could not help but gasp in awe.

"Beautiful, aren't they?" remarked Han noting Ary's reaction. "They reflect her depth of wisdom. Unfortunately for her, they are not an indication of her social charms."

"My dear Han, it is a shame your compassion is not matched by your wit," remarked the blue-winged fairy who then turned toward Ary. "Well, then, young one, have you ever meditated before?"

"I, uh, I, well, um," answered Ary. She was struggling between trying to answer the strange fairy and figuring out what was bothering her. Suddenly, she knew what it was. She had felt the same feeling before at her friend Scarlet's nest.

"I thought not," interrupted Azure. She looked back towards Han and then Ary. "I believe you know the way out.

Blessed Season," she said and then turned to head back to her place in the shadows.

"Blessed Season, indeed!" murmured Han as he turned to go out. But, Ary did not follow him. Instead, she was staring into the shadows in another corner of the room. She looked towards Azure.

"May I...." Ary said timidly. "May I pet him?"

"Pet who?" crackled the old fairy.

Ary pointed into the darkness. "Him!" she said and called to the creature in her mind. From beyond the shadows came a long nose and whiskers followed by the rest of a furry mouse. Ary walked to the mouse and touched its furry nose.

Image 24: Autumn Lake

Han watched Ary pet the mouse and then turned to Azure. "Why, Azure, I never knew you had a pet. You have a soft spot in your heart after all. All that gruff and grimace is just one big act!" he said.

"You can go now, Han!" she grumbled.

Ary turned to go as well but Azure said to her: "No, you stay!"

When Han had flown off into the night sky, Azure led Ary outside.

"Come with me," she said and Ary followed. Outside, the world was dark for night had fallen. Azure turned to Ary.

"Tonight is the Autumn Cross-Quarter, a very sacred night. This is the night when we honor our ancestors and all those who have returned before us. Their bodies are returned to Earth Mother and their souls are returned to Sky Father. Each star we see in the night sky is a reflection of the light of each of our ancestors. Through them we honor the dead," said Azure.

Ary thought back on the death of her friend and mentor Amber. She remembered seeing her body float to the ground and a light that rose from her body. She looked up and chose a star that would honor the memory of her friend and offered it a silent blessing. When she had finished, Azure continued.

"Tonight is also a special night for doing meditation and spiritual work. Come."

Azure and Ary went back inside the cave. Once inside, Azure placed a small cushion on the floor and pointed to it.

"Sit," she said. When Ary had followed her directions, she continued. "Now, I want you to become like one of those stars. I want you to shine bright but be still and silent." Ary sat quietly.

"Relax," said Azure. "You don't have to be stiff. Be firm but pliant like the Great Tree". Azure waited a few moments then continued again. "Now, follow your breath and think of nothing else."

Ary tried to do as she was told but found it hard to do. Her mind kept wandering and thinking about just stopping all this and going away. Every time her mind would start thinking about other things, though, Azure would remind her to listen to her breath and relax. The more she sat, the more she began to feel like she could do it. She also started to sense something else. She felt Azure's presence in her mind as if the old blue-winged fairy could come and sit down inside her head. More than that, she felt the presence of the mouse as well. Each was trying to send her calming thoughts. She began to feel safe and warm and let herself go deep inside. She could feel her mind beginning to focus. She was able to bring her mind back whenever it drifted away. She worked to not focus on her thoughts but on just sitting. So, she sat and she sat and she sat until, suddenly, an image appeared to her.

Ary found herself standing in front of a giant flower. Its petals were long and thick and were reaching out toward her. She could smell its wonderful fragrance and could see its bright colors. She felt drawn toward it and, so, she walked closer to it. She went beyond the petals and sought to look inside its middle section but as she started to get closer, the petals of the flower curled in from behind her and pushed her towards the center of the flower. Ary heard herself scream as she was forced into the center of the flower but, when she reached what should have been a solid foundation, she found herself trapped inside the flower itself. It was like being inside a tunnel that got more narrow as you continued inside.

She didn't know how, but there was just enough light on the inside for Ary to see where she was going. Since she couldn't turn around and go back, she started walking down the dark green tunnel. It got thinner and thinner until she had to crawl to continue. She got to a point where she thought she could go no further but as she stuck her head into the thin tunnel she saw that there was a larger space beyond. The walls around her were flexible so she knew she could squeeze herself into the space. She struggled and strained to get through and finally managed to work her way beyond the hole. She slipped down and landed on another dark green surface. After she stood and righted herself, she noticed a window at the edge of the space. She walked over to it and peered out. From there, she could see the stalk and distant flower from which she had first been swallowed up. She saw other flowers as well. They each seemed to wave and dance in the wind but each was connected to the place where she now found herself.

Ary tried to get the window open any way that she could but it did not budge. She looked around the strange room but there was no way out. She started to worry that she would not be able to find any way out at all but before she could think about it much more, strange brown roots began to pop up from the floor of the room. Each jutted straight up. It started with just a few, but more and more pushed their way through the surface. They started to surround her and, before she knew it, they were circling her feet and pulling her down. The floor became a loose mass of dirt and Ary felt herself being pulled down into the ground. She screamed and tried to fight what was happening to her but with little success. The strange roots encircled her legs and pulled her down all the way into the dirt floor. She was afraid that she would suffocate in the dirt but she did not.

Instead, she found herself in a vast cavern of dirt and roots that ran tangled and twisted in all directions. She saw the root structure of every plant and tree and bush that lived on the ground of the Forest of Songs. Each root was gently twisting and moving around. It was hard to tell which one belonged to which plant. It was one giant underground structure of roots and dirt. The roots around her legs released their grip but Ary was still trapped and unable to climb her way out. Frustrated and frightened, she broke down and just began to cry.

Several moments went by when, suddenly, Ary heard a sound above her. She looked up only to have dirt fall down upon her. Then, there appeared a hand that had pushed through the dirt and was reaching for her. She grabbed the hand firmly and it pulled her gently out of the hole. When she had reached the surface, she gasped. Standing before her was the image of her old departed friend, Amber.

"Amber!" she cried as she hugged her mentor. "But I thought you were gone!"

"I will always be with you in your dreams," Amber said as she continued to hold the young fairy. "Did you remember what I last told you?" she whispered.

"Be kind. Be considerate. Be true." Ary replied.

"Yes. Be kind: do not bring harm to yourself or others. Be considerate: respect those people and things that you and others love. Be true: be true to yourself and others. This is the way of the fairies and what you have seen here is the reason why."

"I don't understand, Amber."

"You will," said Amber and she held Ary close to her.

After another moment, Amber took Ary by the shoulders and looked her into the face. "It is time for you to return, now," she said.

Ary let a tear of joy fall from her face and then, knowing her friend was right, said: "How do I do that?"

"Sit, and relax," said Amber. Ary did as she was told while Amber continued.

"Focus on your breath," she said. "Focus on your breath, focus on your breath."

Ary breathed gently and followed the air as it moved in and out of her body. She let go of her thoughts.

"Focus on your breath," Ary heard the words again but this time it was the voice of Azure that spoke them. Ary opened her eyes and found herself back in the old fairy's den. Instead of the same old crotchety face Ary had seen on her before, however, the brilliant blue-winged fairy was smiling at her.

"Blessed Season!" said Azure. "Now, go home and think about what you have seen."

The old fairy said nothing else and retreated slowly and gracefully back into the shadows from where she had come. The mouse came to Ary and snuggled its nose into her arm. Ary pet her head gently on the top of its head. She felt a good feeling coming from the mouse and gave it a gentle squeeze before standing up, stretching her wings, and then going outside of the cave into the night.

$\mathcal{S}$tory no. 12
Cerise Gets Carried Away

Arylide was a young yellow-winged fairy who lived on a branch of the Great Tree at the edge of the Forest of Songs. These are the stories of her first year.

Image 25: The Cat

It was late Autumn in the Forest of Songs and all the leaves had blown off the trees and covered the ground in a thick crunchy carpet. The days had started to grow cold and short in light but not cold enough to keep the fairies from playing. Ary and her friends decided to spend the day frolicking in the sunlight. They were playing tag by flying fast and furious among the trees. One of them would try and tag another while zipping between branches and twigs. The fact that there were no leaves on the trees gave them a lot more space for maneuvering while flying. Careful control and attention, however, were needed to keep from hitting the trees while moving fast and turning quick. If that wasn't challenging enough, the late Autumn winds made it even harder to fly without hitting anything. Hard gusts of wind could suddenly blow through the woods at any time and send one of the fairies flying in a new direction.

At one point in the game, Ary managed to avoid a tag by her fast flying friend Cerise and turned quickly away to escape. Cerise caught a glimpse of their red-winged friend Scarlet surrounded by a small flock of chickadees who wanted to play with Scarlet as well. Cerise darted in the direction of Scarlet but lost sight of her, blocked by the birds who were flying nearby. Ary seized the opportunity to dive down close to the ground to find a place to hide. She found a place where two tree trunks came together into a V shape and landed in the middle of them. Just then, a strong gust of wind blew through the Forest. Ary held on to the bark of one of the trees. She heard a muffled scream and saw Scarlet blow by in a red blur. Ary thought her friend was going to be carried off into a tree trunk and she prepared herself to fly in her friend's direction and try to catch her but before she had a chance to take off, a blue jay whirled from behind a tree and carefully grasped Scarlet in its claws. It gently set Scarlet down on the ground near where Ary was watching. Ary waved her arms so that Scarlet would see her.

"Psst! Scarlet! Over here!" Ary said, trying to be quiet so that Cerise might not hear her. Scarlet was gently touching the beak of the blue jay to thank it when she saw Ary. She flew over to her.

"You almost crashed into that tree," said Ary.

"I wasn't too worried," shrugged Scarlet. "That blue jay was hoping to join in the game. Besides, I would probably just have bounced off that tree and kept on flying."

Overhead, Cerise flew past them calling their names. It was obvious that she wanted to keep chasing them. Ary and Scarlet ducked behind the tree trunk to avoid detection. Cerise's voice faded into the distance.

"Should we fly after Cerise?" asked Ary but Scarlet put her fingers to her lips.

"Shh!" hushed Scarlet. "I sense something nearby."

Ary got quiet and focused on her feelings. When she opened herself up, she began to feel a presence as well. She couldn't tell if the creature posed a danger or not. Just then, a dark figure appeared from behind the other side of the tree trunk where they were hiding. From the shadows, the face of a black cat suddenly appeared before them. It made a hissing sound at the two fairies that frightened Ary but not her friend. Scarlet stayed calm and put out her hand. Ary could feel an outpouring of care and compassion from within Scarlet. The cat sniffed Scarlet's tiny hand and then relaxed. Scarlet pet the creature's head as the cat moved closer. Ary could even hear it purr a little.

"It wants to play, too," said Scarlet softly.

Just then, the two fairies heard the voice of Cerise just behind and above them.

"There you are, now I..." began Cerise, but before she could finish, the cat leapt up to catch Cerise as if to play with her. Cerise was caught off guard and tried to turn and fly away. She managed to get around but, before she could get away, the tip of the cat's claw ripped through part of

Cerise's right wing. Cerise started to spin uncontrollably downwards and would have landed on the soft leaves on the ground but, instead, another strong gust picked her up and carried her off.

"Cerise is in trouble!" cried Ary and prepared to jump into the wind to catch her but Scarlet grabbed her arm. "There might be a faster way," said Scarlet as she approached the black cat. She touched the top of the creature's head and closed her eyes.

"He'll do it," she said softly. Then, she jumped onto the back of the cat.

Image 26: The House In The Woods

"C'mon!" she called out to her friend. Ary flew up to the cat and climbed on its back behind Scarlet. They each grabbed a handful of fur and held on. The cat took off in the direction that Cerise had been blown away. The cat was strong and fast and Ary and Scarlet had to use all their own strength to hang on.

The dark feline darted between trees, logs, stumps, and rocks as he ran. Several times he had to jump to get over fallen debris and the two fairies on its back struggled to keep from getting thrown off. It ran and ran and, together, they went further into the woods than either fairy had ever been. As they continued, Ary was able to occasionally get a glimpse of Cerise as she was struggling to get control of her damaged wing so she could fly again but it was no use. She alternated between swirling towards the ground and being carried away by strong gusts.

Eventually, the cat reached the far edge of the Forest and suddenly stopped just as Cerise was picked up by another strong gust of wind and flew over their heads. Ary and Scarlet turned to see where she was headed and were surprised to see several houses beyond the edge of the woods. They realized that they were at the end of the Forest of Songs - a place where very few fairies ever ventured because it was where the humans lived.

Ary and Scarlet saw Cerise being blown toward the window of an upstairs bedroom and heard her body hit the glass. It was not a hard hit because the wind started to die down just as she got near the window, but the strike was hard enough to cause Cerise to fall and land on the ledge below the window.

"C'mon," said Scarlet as she patted the head of the cat to thank it but Ary noticed something.

"Wait!" said Ary as they heard a sound coming from the house. The window where Cerise had landed had just opened. A human boy looked out of the window and noticed the barely moving fairy below it. Ary looked at the boy carefully. She thought she had seen him before. Then, she remembered. He was the boy she had once seen looking at her during the Summer Solstice. She didn't know it then but she sensed now that this human was a kind one. They both watched as the boy scooped up Cerise and took her inside the house. Without saying a word, the other two fairies flew up to the window and looked in - careful to not be seen.

Inside the room, Ary and Scarlet saw the boy gently put the fairy down. As he placed her on a stack of soft tissues, Cerise started to become more conscious. At first she was afraid of the boy and was too scared to move. Then, she noticed that the boy meant her no harm and, so, she started to relax. The boy was trying to talk to her but none of the fairies could understand what he was saying. He offered her a drop of water from a small spoon and she drank.

Another gust of wind blew through the room and brought the attention of the boy towards the window. He was surprised to see the other two fairies crouching there. He motioned for them to come in. They looked at each other and then flew in to check on their friend. The boy stepped back so that he would not frighten them. Ary and Scarlet hugged Cerise and asked if she was all right. It was then that Ary noticed a strange sound but could not see where it was coming from. She decided to ignore it so that she could help her friend.

"I think with a little rest to let my wing heal that I will be fine. That human helped me," she said pointing to the boy.

Ary flew up and headed towards the boy. She tried to say thank you but he obviously did not understand her strange language so she flew to his cheek and gave him a soft kiss. The boy's face turned red and Ary knew he understood.

"We saw the human help you from the window," said Scarlet. She turned towards Ary. "Ary, come and help me carry her back to her nest."

"Sure," replied Ary and she started flying in the direction of her friends but then she heard the strange sound again coming from the distance. It was a soft but awful sound and it greatly bothered her.

"Wait!" Ary called out as she stopped to listen to figure out the direction of the sound. When she did, she decided to find out what was causing it. She pointed herself toward the disturbance and began to fly. She left the boy's room and headed through other rooms until she reached the other side of the house. The boy decided to follow but could not keep up with her. Ary reached a window that faced out in the exact opposite direction from where the fairies had come. There she stopped and looked at what was happening outside. The humans and their machines were clearing out some trees to make room for another building.

Ary froze in utter horror at what she was seeing. A large bulldozer was pushing over whole trees and any other plant that got in its way. She could only imagine all the creatures that had run away in horror at the terrible sights and sounds of this destruction. Ary turned away and started to cry. She couldn't stand to watch it any longer. The boy came into the room behind her and ran to the window to see what the young fairy was upset about. He looked into the fairy's small eyes and then outside. Ary had a feeling that the human boy understood her. There was a look in his eye that seemed to say he was looking differently at what was happening.

Ary could stand the sounds from beyond the window no longer. She took one last look at the boy and then turned to fly back to her friends. She flew back through the rooms from where she had come and found Scarlet trying to lift Cerise up but she was struggling. Ary flew over to her friends and helped Scarlet pick up Cerise. They both knew that Cerise's wing would eventually heal on its own but, for now, she would need their help to get back. Once the three of them got back into the cover of the Forest, Scarlet could call upon her animal friends to help out, but none would dare come so close to a human house without some kind of cover.

When Ary and Scarlet had lifted Cerise up together, they carefully flew her out of the house and into the edge of the Forest of Songs.

Story no. 13
The Bulldozer Comes to the Forest of Songs

Arylide was a young yellow-winged fairy who lived on a branch of the Great Tree at the edge of the Forest of Songs. These are the stories of her first year.

Image 27: The Bulldozer

It was the first day of Winter. The days had become quite cold and every day it seemed like it was getting ready to snow. Some snow flurries had come during the past few weeks but no snow had yet covered the ground for any long period of time.

It was especially cold in the early morning hours and, usually, fairies made a point of sleeping in during cold winter mornings but this particular morning was a special one. Today was the Winter Solstice and during the dark and chilly hours before the first rays of the sun broke on the horizon, many of the fairies that lived in and around the Great Tree flew up to the highest branches of the tree and huddled together to stay warm. They would wait to see the sun rise over the land because they knew that, after the Solstice, the days would become longer and the warmth and light of the sun would soon return. It was a bittersweet day because although the sun's light and strength was returning, this day also signaled the beginning of the Winter season.

On this night , the fairies lit torches to help them find their way to the top of the tree and to help provide some much needed warmth. The great Tree became alive with tiny moving lights that flickered all up and down its mighty trunk. Normally, such a dazzling display would have attracted the unwanted attention of the humans but, since they often had lights on their own houses, few took notice of the tiny glow around the Great Tree. Those that might see them would simply think they were fireflies.

Ary and her friends Scarlet and Cerise huddled together on a high branch and tried to keep each other warm. They placed their small torches on a nearby branch. Around them were most of the other fairies that lived near the Great Tree. They managed to keep themselves relatively warm by staying close to their torches and by fluttering their wings to fan the warm air toward each other The effect of all that flapping was to create a low buzzing sound that became the drone pitch for their chanting and singing as the sun slowly started to break light into the darkness.

"Look," said Ary, excitedly pointing toward the first golden rays of light in the distance.

"It's about time!" said Cerise with chattering teeth.

Scarlet put her arms around her friend and tried to warm her up.

"It won't be much longer now. Grandfather Sun will be reborn today and then we can move into the cave and be warm," Scarlet said softly.

For weeks, the fairies had been preparing for their time underground. Every year at this time, they moved their sparse belongings down into a set of underground chambers near the Great Tree and lived together there until the first signs of Spring. Ary, of course, had the hardest time getting ready for Winter because she had so many books to store but her friends had managed to help her. After the Solstice, they would all be ready to stay warm and dry under the ground for a while.

As the light of the sun began painting the morning sky in brilliant colors, the chanting and the humming sound got softer until there was hardly any sound at all. All the fairies nearly held their breath in a state of deep reverence as they waited for the first appearance of the round yellow sun. When the glorious light rose up to brighten the sky, the fairies cheered amd began their chanting yet again.

Ary, Scarlet, and Cerise hugged each other in the red-orange light and sat down together. Each of them had made their own gifts to give each other. Usually, those gifts were things that the fairies had made to help others get through the long period under the ground, but Scarlet just enjoyed making and sharing beautiful things. She started the gift-giving.

"Here, Ary. Here, Cerise," she said handing them each an intricately designed small painting. Both of them were delighted at the beautiful design and creativity that went into the gift.

"Thank you," said Cerise almost speechless.

"It's so beautiful," remarked Ary. "I will put it up and admire it every day."

Cerise went next and handed each of her friends a bowl that she had made by interlacing small twigs together. She had some artistic talent but it certainly did not match that of Scarlet's so she focused on making things that were useful. Both Ary and Scarlet appreciated the gift and told her thet they would be sure to use them at the very next meal.

Finally, it was Ary's turn to offer a gift to her friends. But, instead of handing them a present, Ary just looked down toward the ground in sadness.

"What is it, Ary?" asked Cerise.

Ary let out a heavy sigh and then looked sadly at her two friends. "Oh, both of you have given me such wonderful gifts and I don't really have anything like them to give to you. I've been so busy trying to get my books written and do my various studies that I have had no time to make either of you something. I'm sorry."

"Oh, Ary," said Scarlet. "You don't need to make us anything. You give us so much by just being our friend."

"That's right," agreed Cerise.

"Oh, you too are the best friends a fairy could have," said Ary. She pulled out a couple of very small books out from under her tunic.

"I did find two copies of poetry from a little known but very good poet. This could be good reading during the winter time."

Both Cerise and Scarlet took the tiny books and flipped through them.

"These are beautiful," exclaimed Cerise. Scarlet nodded in agreement.

Just then the purple-winged fairy Han flew above them.

"It's time to go, fairies!" he said to them and then flew away. He had been put in charge of getting all the fairies into the caves for the Winter.

"Come on. We better get going," said Ary.

Image 28: The Forest in the Snow

The three fairies collected their gifts and their torches and headed down the length of the tall tree towards the ground. They had already established places below where they would be staying. Of course, being close friends, they had chosen to share a space. Unlike the Great Tree, the space was limited underground.

When the three had reached one of the entrances to the underground chambers, they found a rock to sit on while letting many of the others go in first. As they sat and watched the parade of fairies go by, the skies above started to cloud up and the sun appeared between floating dark masses.

Scarlet looked up. "Looks like we will be going in just in time," she said. By then, most of the fairies had gone underground.

"We better go on in," said Cerise. She and Scarlet rose up to head toward the entrance but noticed that Ary was not moving. She had a strange look on her face.

"Ary," said Cerise. "They're going to close the entrances soon."

Ary did not move. She had her ears cocked up as if she were trying to listen to something. In fact, Ary wasn't sure, but she thought she did hear a sound and it frightened her. She listened to find out if she had been mistaken.

"What is it?" asked Scarlet.

"I thought I heard something," whispered Ary.

The three fairies waited for a few moments. Then, Ary looked up in fear.

"There!" she whispered. "Did you hear it?"

The other two looked at each other in confusion but then Cerise began to hear something too. It was faint and in the distance but it was unmistakeable. Scarlet looked at Cerise. She had heard it too.

"No, it can't be!" Ary cried as she flew off in the direction of the sound as fast as she could. Scarlet looked at Cerise and called out "Tell the others!" before she went out after Ary. When Ary had gone nearly to the edge of the woods, she stopped at a tree, looked ahead, and saw what she most feared. There, at the edge of the Forest of Songs and moving toward them was the bulldozer she had seen when she had found herself in the home of a human boy. It was tearing up the trees and plants as it moved forward.

"No!" cried out Ary but she knew it was no use. She was no match against that great yellow monster. As she watched it move toward her slowly and methodically, other fairies began to join her. Each one fell silent in shock as they realized what was happening.

There were also other humans who had appeared to see what was going on. Normally, the fairies would be worried about being seen by the humans but the shock of watching this destruction of their beloved forest took away that fear. Ary saw the humans as they looked on and noticed that they did not seem to care so much about what was happening. They were looking on more in curiosity than in horror. But, there was one human that seemed to show concern on his face. It was the human boy that the three fairies had encountered just a few weeks ago. Ary caught a glimpse of him.

"Look," whispered Ary pointing in the direction of the boy.

"Quick!" said Scarlet. "Concentrate on sending him your thoughts - just like we have done with the animals. He may still be young enough to sense it."

"What do we send him?" Asked Ary.

"The body of Earth Mother is sacred, like all bodies," she said. But, remember," Scarlet reminded them. "You need to feel it in your heart as you send the idea to him!"

Ary, Cerise, and Scarlet all reached down into their hearts and thought about the sacredness of their own bodies. They knew they did not want others touching or hurting them and they extended those feelings to the body of Earth Mother. They then extended those feelings toward the young human boy in the distance. They held him in their heart as well and tried to fill him with the same feelings they were now experiencing. The other fairies who had gathered nearby tried hurling stones and rocks at the bulldozer but to no avail. Others who were near Ary and her friends figured out what they were doing and joined in with the meditation.

At one point, Ary looked toward the human boy and thought she saw him react to their efforts. He looked directly in her direction and then looked at the yellow machine that was plowing down the trees. She could almost feel a connection in her heart with the young boy, but then the boy turned and ran away.

Ary sighed and said: "Oh, it's no use."

Cerise and Scarlet turned towards their friend and then saw the boy run off away from the woods. They, too, felt frustration and disappointment.

"What do we do now?" whispered Scarlet.

"I've seen this machine in action," grumbled Ary. It destroys everything in its way. There's no stopping it. We have to get to the Great Tree and save what we can and then we will have to find another forest to live in - one without humans."

"Is there such a place anymore?" asked Cerise.

"I don't know," sighed Ary.

Together, the three of them watched the yellow monster devour the woods bit by bit as it inched towards them. Ary looked at her two friends.

"C'mon, let's go while we can," she said and started to head toward home.

But, before she could take off, Scarlet shouted. "Wait! Look!" She was pointing in the direction where the boy had left. There, in the distance, the boy appeared again and with him were several other humans. Ary guessed they may have been his family and friends. The boy was pulling a couple of them with his hands while others followed him close behind. The small band of humans ran to a spot in front of the bulldozer and stood there shouting and screaming. All the other fairies hovered and watched. They could not believe what they were seeing. The bulldozer stopped moving and a human came up from within it. He also was shouting and screaming but the yellow beast no longer moved. There was a lot more shouting and screaming but, eventually, everyone calmed downor walked away in anger. The bulldozer was abandoned where it stopped and the humans all left - all, that is, except one. The young boy remained behind and headed toward where the fairies were watching. When the fairies realized where he was headed, they got ready to fly back towards the caves by the Great Tree.

"Ary, let's go!" said Cerise.

"You two go ahead. I'll meet you there in a moment," said Ary. Cerise and Scarlet flew away but Ary remained.

Within a few moments, the boy had come near to where Ary was waiting in a tree branch. The boy had guessed where the fairies had been but could not see Ary watching him. Ary softly flew down and hovered in front of him. The boy put his hand out and Ary landed on it. She looked at him and said 'thank you.' Though she knew he could not understand her words, she thought that he might get the feelings that she sent with the words. After she had spoken, the boy looked at her and then smiled. Ary smiled back. Then, she lifted off from his hands and flew off.

Ary flew back towards the Great Tree and headed toward one of the entrances to the underground caves. Cerise and Scarlet were at the entrance waiting for her. Together, the three flew into the cave while other fairies worked to close the entrance against the cold. As they worked, small flakes of snow began to drift down upon the floor of the Forest of Songs.

Story no. 14
Percy's Machine

Arylide was a young yellow-winged fairy who lived on a branch of the Great Tree at the edge of the Forest of Songs. These are the stories of her first year.

Image 29: The Underground Cave

It was early Winter and the fairies were all underground in a collection of chambers dug out to help them survive the cold. There they would remain until the first signs of Spring appeared and they could go back to living in the Great Tree.

For many fairies, living in the underground caves was a chance to spend most of the day sleeping, eating, reading, or doing other quiet and relaxing activities but the younger fairies had a hard time staying still for so many weeks. They often had to invent games that they could play in the torch lit caverns.

Ary, Cerise, and Scarlet were doing just that. They had formed together a ball made from dried leaves and sap and were playing in the very back portion of the caves where few went so that they would not disturb the others. They took turns throwing and catching the ball and, of course, were laughing and calling out as they went. They made sure that they had brought plenty of torches with them so that they would have a lot of light. Otherwise, they would have been covered
in darkness.

The more they played, the less they began to notice how deep and far they had gone into the caves. They just kept throwing the ball and trying to catch it no matter where it landed. These caves had been built by moles, mice, and other creatures and went for long distances. The fairies had relayed to these creatures that they would help bring them food for the Winter if they would let the fairies live in a certain section of the caves. The three young female fairies had long passed that invisible barrier and were unknowingly entering into the other territory. Now, they had come to a place that they did not know.

"Where are we?" asked Ary as she picked up the ball that had been thrown into a dark corner. She held a torch in one hand and the ball in the other hand and landed.

"I'm not sure," said Scarlet looking around. She pointed down a corridor. "But I think we came from that way."

"C'mon, Cerise," said Ary looking in another direction. Cerise was peering down a small passageway with her torch. Ary flew over to her.

"What is it, Cerise?"

Cerise continued to peer down the dark passageway. "I sense a presence here," she said.

Ary concentrated on her feelings and then sensed something as well but it was not very strong. She knew Cerise was much better at this.

"It's not threatening?" Ary asked.

"No," said Cerise. It wants to be a friend but I think it is trying to tell me something. I just can't make it out." Cerise had to crawl to get into the small space and she started to work her way in.

"Are you sure you want to do that?" Ary questioned.

Cerise turned back to Ary. "I think it is frightened by my torch," she said and then blew out her torch against the advice of Ary.

Just then Scarlet came over to them and landed near Ary.

"What's going on?" Scarlet asked Ary.

Scarlet turned to look down the small passageway. "C'mon, Cerise. That doesn't look safe."

"Scarlet, put your torch down! You're scaring it," said Cerise.

"Scaring what?" asked Scarlet. But before she could get a response, a mole stuck its nose out of the ground not in the passageway but from an even smaller hole that was near where Ary and Scarlet were now standing. The two standing fairies suddenly noticed the nose at their legs and were surprised. Both let out a little scream while Scarlet jumped up and landed in the entrance of the passageway where Cerise was looking. The combination of the screams and the force of Scarlet's jump caused Cerise to slip. A portion of the passage gave way and opened up below Cerise. She tried to hang on and grab anything she could find but she was in the dark since she had blown out her torch and she could not see well enough to find something to hang onto. Cerise fell into another passageway which held an underground stream.

Ary and Scarlet heard their friend scream and then they heard a splashing sound. They looked at each other in horror. Without saying a word, the two took their torches and went in after her. They managed to squeeze through the hole in the small tunnel. Ary held on to Scarlet as she went through the hole so that she could get her wings through and not fall to the bottom. That way Scarlet could hover below the opening and help Ary come through.

There was enough room around the underground stream to let the fairies fly but they knew Cerise would still be in trouble because fairies cannot fly if their wings get wet. Fairies can do a decent job of swimming if they have to, but wet wings make it difficult to maneuver in the water. Ary and Cerise listened and heard the sound of splashing and cries of help further down the stream. They flew towards the sounds and saw their friend struggling in the water.

"Don't panic, Cerise," Ary called out while she flew as close as she could to reassure her friend. She tried to grab her friens hand and pull her out but Cerise was moving about too wildly.

Scarlet searched for a branch and found one to the side of the stream. She picked it up and flew over until she was in front of Cerise. She then dropped the branch into the water. Cerise managed to grab it and hang on. Once secure on the log, Cerise kicked her legs and moved to the side of the stream to a soft open spot where she was able to get out of the water. Ary and Scarlet moved close to Cerise and brought their torches close to her so that she could get warm and dry.

"Thank you both," said Cerise.

The fairies all took a moment to catch their breath.

"I figured out what the creature was trying to tell me," said Cerise as her teeth chattered and she panted.

"What was that?" asked Ary.

"It was trying to tell me that the passageway wasn't safe," stammered Cerise.

"Couldn't you figure that out before you went tumbling into the water?" huffed Scarlet.

"Well, if you hadn't come crashing into me and screaming like some screech owl then..." Cerise stopped in mid sentence and listened. "Oh my," she said. "I must be worse off than I thought. I'm hearing bells."

"No, I thought I heard something too," Ary whispered.

The three sat very quietly for several moments but heard nothing. They sat some more but still there was nothing but the sound of the running water near them.

Scarlet stood up. "Both of you are nuts!" she said. "Your wings should be almost dry, Cerise. We should go."

The other two fairies stood up and dusted themselves off. Scarlet fluttered her wings and hovered above them. Then, suddenly all three of them heard the bell sound. It was far off and very faint but it was clear. Ary and Cerise turned and looked up at Scarlet.

"Yea, I heard it that time," she whispered.

Cerise fluttered her wings gently and let the air finish drying them off.

"Ok, Cerise?" Ary said softly.

Cerise nodded and the three of them lifted gently over the water and headed toward the sound of the bell. They continued to head downstream with their two torches ablaze. After a few moments of following the water, they saw a light in the distance. Scarlet pointed and they all headed toward it. The light became slightly brighter and larger as they approached. Soon, the light became the entrance to another cave. The three fairies looked at each other. They knew they were quite lost and would probably need help to find their way out. They knew they would need to see what or who was in that cave and hope that he or she could help them. They flew into the cave.

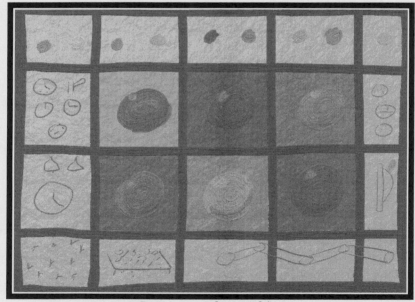

Image 30: The Machine

When they got inside they saw a small chamber lit with several torches. Instead of hearing bells, however, they heard the sound of snoring. They looked toward the direction from which the snoring was coming. In the corner of the room on a small cot made of leaves and twigs was a thin and frail fairy who was sleeping. The three fairies landed softly on the ground.

"Should we wake him?" Scarlet whispered.

"I'm not sure," said Cerise. He might get angry or be grumpy and kick us out."

"But we need his help," Ary said softly.

Just then a bell went off in another chamber behind the sleeping fairy. It was the same sound they had heard in the distance but now it was much louder and clearer. At its chime, the male fairy leaped out of bed and went running into the chamber from which the bell had just sounded. He was in such a hurry that he didn't even notice the three fairies standing in his front chamber.

Ary, Cerise, and Scarlet looked at each other but dared not move. Shortly afterwards, the strange male fairy came slowly back into the room where they were standing. He was looking downward and seem tired and worn out. He had almost reached his cot again when he did finally notice the females standing there watching him. When he did see them, he jumped and screamed which caused the three female fairies to jump and scream as well. The strange male fairy ducked again into the back room. After he disappeared, Ary took a few steps into the center of the room.

"Excuse me!" she called out. "We're not here to hurt you. We just need to talk to you."

The face of the male fairy peered around the corner and looked at them.

"Well, I'm not scared," the face said. "I, uh, I was uh, just checking on my machine." He stepped out into the room.

"I'm Arylide and these are my friends Cerise and Scarlet."

"Pleased to meet you," he said with a deep bow and a long swing of one of his arms across his chest. "I am Perssimon but you can just call me Percy. Are you here to help me with my machine?" he asked.

"Well, uh, no," stammered Ary.

"We're here to ask if you can help us get back to the other fairies," said Cerise as she and Scarlet moved up next to Ary.

"Well, uh, yes! I can do that," he said. "I can certainly do that." He moved into the chamber and started waving his arms all around. "Oh yes, that certainly is easy to do. In fact, I even have a map around here somewhere."

The curious fairy started moving about the room turning over papers and leaves and branches obviously looking for the map he just mentioned. It was then that the three female fairies noticed the orange color that tinged the male fairy's wings. Before he could finish his search, however, another bell sound went off in the back room. When he heard that, he dropped what he was doing and ran quickly back to the other room and disappeared. The three female fairies looked at each other in bewilderment.

"I have to see what is going on back there," said Scarlet.

"No, don't!" begged Cerise but Scarlet started slowly walking to the back room. When she got to the corner, she peered around and then turned back toward her friends.

"Come on!" said Scarlet. "You've got to see this!" She disappeared around the corner.

Ary looked at Cerise and grabbed her elbow. Together, they went toward the back room and followed Scarlet. When Ary rounded the corner into that next room, she saw something that was simply amazing. There, in front of them was a gigantic machine that stretched along the back wall of the room. There were things on it that spun and moved and twisted and whirred. Percy was at the machine and he was spinning one of the many colored globes that were built into it.

Just then, another bell went off next to yet another brightly colored orb that was starting to slow down. Percy quickly ran over to that orb and gave it several good spins with his hands until it was twirling furiously like the others. He turned around and noticed the three fairies and, of course, let out another scream. Again, he frightened the fairies and they, in turn, screamed as well.

"You frightened me," he said.

"We're sorry," said Ary but she was still staring at the machine. Percy saw her gaze and then suddenly lit up.

"Pretty amazing, isn't it?" he asked.

"It sure is," murmured Scarlet.

To Ary, the machine was a fascinating collection of moving parts but to Scarlet, it was a work of art in motion. Cerise, however, was less impressed. She was a lover of living beings. Machines meant little to her.

"What is this thing?" cracked Cerise.

"It's a machine to keep the world running," beamed Percy as he proudly strutted back and forth in front of his handiwork. "As long as the wheels spin and the parts move, this machine helps keep the world moving smoothly and keeps all creatures happy. The bells are here to remind me to spin these orbs when they start to slow down. If they slow down they will stop spinning Unfortunately, I don't get much sleep because of that but I do have an important job to do!"

Cerise just stared at him in disbelief until she finally spoke: "That's crazy," she said.

Percy either didn't hear her or just ignored her and kept talking. "You see, there was a time when the winters were longer and colder and fairies did not treat each other with respect and dignity like they do now so I decided that I needed to do something to help the world. It was then that I made this masterpiece - my life's work." Percy then sat down on the floor. "Oh, it does make me tired, though. I keep hoping that, someday, someone will come to help me out. I thought you might be my helpers."

"Couldn't you use water power, or wind power, or fire and steam to help you push all those wheels around," Scarlet questioned the orange-winged fairy.

Percy jumped up and wagged his finger in Scarlet's direction. "Ah! Ah-ha-ha!" he thundered. "Then the machine would belong to the elements! Oh, no, no, no. It is MY machine and I must keep it running."

"But, how do you know this machine really does what you say it does?" asked Ary.

Percy flashed Ary a strange smile. "I do NOT know, but I BELIEVE it with all my heart that it does."

"But what if your belief is false?" quipped Cerise.

The face of the curious male fairy twisted up. "I believe it is true and that is all that matters!" he roared but then softened his tone. "This machine is my life. It is what gives me purpose and meaning. I ask that you at least respect that!"

The three female fairies fell silent while they considered Percy's words. Ary continued to stare at the machine in wonderment. She watched the many spinning multi-colored orbs and all the other moving parts. There were shiny cogs and levers. She could tell that each had been individually handmade and decorated. There were handles and knobs and springs and dials and wheels and wheels within wheels and wheels that moved other wheels. And, of course, there were bells. She saw how all the individual parts each had its own function but worked together. She saw how it all flowed within itself in one consistent grand motion. It was all so elegant and poetic.

Then, something inside Ary's mind flashed like a bolt of lightning on a summer night. Suddenly, everything made sense: Amber's words, the struggle of her wings, sensing other creatures, and the strange dream about the flowers. It all came together and Ary understood. She smiled.

Percy broke the silence.

"Well, then. Let's get you three back to your home. Now where is that map?" he bubbled and started again on his search for his map. Finally, after several moments of tossing around papers and other debris, he found a certain piece of paper. "Here it is!" he burst.

Percy handed the piece of paper to Cerise. The three female fairies got together and looked it over. On it was a drawing of the caves but it was rough and confusing.

"What is this?" asked Scarlet.

"Oh well, yes," said Percy. "I suppose it may be discombobulated. I drew it from my memory. I used to explore these caves long before I built my machine. You can take that with you. I'll draw another one when you go. Here!" he exclaimed as he took the map from Cerise and then explained how to use it. He began marking on it while they watched.

"We are here," he began. "Follow this way along the creek and then go this way and this way. When you get here, just continue straight on to the fairies lair. There!"

"Thank you," said Ary. "We'll ask if anyone would like to come and help you with your machine when we get back."

131

"Thank you!" said Percy as he gave them another long and formal bow. With that, the three female fairies grabbed their torches, took the map, and turned to fly out of the bizarre fairy's cave. With the help of Percy's map, they made their way back.

𝒮tory no. 15
The Lighting

Arylide was a deep golden-winged fairy who lived on a branch of the Great Tree at the edge of the Forest of Songs. These are the stories of her first year.

Image 31: Arylide with Yellow Wings

It was the height of Winter and the Forest of Songs were covered in snow. The air was cold and the nights were bitter but the fairies were able to stay warm in their underground Winter caverns. This was the time of the year when they took advantage of the time underground to get a lot of rest and relaxation. Though they did not exactly hibernate, but they did become much less active than they usually were in the days of Summer. As the number of days increased as they stayed underground, things started to get a little difficult. Food supplies started to get thin and some of the fairies got eager to return to the sunlight and open air. Some even ventured out into the frigid air to be outside but could only stand to be out for a very short time. Flying was very difficult in frigid air.

Ary took advantage of the season to catch up on her reading. She particularly enjoyed reading works that caused her to think about things or to see things in a new way. She was jotting down some notes concerning one of the books she was reading when she suddenly stopped and looked up. She felt something within her but was unsure what it could be. She cleared her mind and let images come to her on their own time. She saw her friend Scarlet in her mind and she did not look well. Scarlet was calling out to her. Ary immediately put her book down and jumped up. Scarlet was in trouble but wasn't exactly sure where she was. She closed her eyes and concentrated again. She started moving her wings and lifted off the ground. She let her heart guide her. She felt which direction was the right way and then she opened her eyes again and flew in that direction. She flew down different pathways sometimes going the wrong way until, eventually, she found her way to Scarlet.

The red-winged fairy was lying down on the ground in a dark corner of the fairy lair and looked terrible.

"Oh, this is it, this is it! I'm done for, I know it!" she complained.

"Scarlet, what is it?" pleaded Ary.

"I don't know. All of a sudden I just got so tired and weak. It must be my time. Oh, this is terrible," moaned Scarlet.

"I've got to get you some help," said Ary but even before she could get the words out, they both heard the sound of wings. It was Cerise coming to help.

"Oh, good. It's Cerise," said Ary.

"Oh, Cerise!" cried Scarlet. "You've been such a good friend and now you've come to see me in my final hour," she said with great dramatics.

Cerise took a close look at her friend Scarlet. She then peered into her friend's eyes. "This is not your time, Scarlet," she said. "You're just suffering from light deprivation."

"Light deprivation! That sounds awful! Is it contagious?" asked Scarlet as she covered her mouth.

"My goodness, no!" remarked Cerise trying not to laugh. "It comes from being underground too long and not getting enough light."

"Is there anything we can do for her?" asked Ary.

"Well," thought Cerise. "She's a little too weak to take outside in the cold. We need to find a window for her but there aren't any windows down here." Cerise knew that there were plenty of small air vents throughout the caves but there were no light windows.

"Could we build one for her?" asked Ary.

"Well," thought Cerise. "Maybe, but we're going to need some help."

"Kelly!" pronounced Ary. "I'll go see if I can find him," she said.

"I'll stay here with Scarlet," said Cerise.

With that, Ary flew off into the caverns and searched for her green-winged friend Kelly. She came across many different fairies whose wings were all different colors. Some wings were brigthly colored and some were almost transparent. Most were reading or talking quietly together but she didn't find any green-winged fairies at all. After searching for quite some time she came around a corner and heard a sound. It was racous and musical. Ary decided to follow the sound and was lead to a brightly lit room. Inside were a large number of green-winged fairies. They were dancing, singing, playing instruments, and just having a great time. Ary landed at the edge of the gathering.

"Those crazy green fairies," Ary whispered lovingly under her breath. "They are always in motion!"

She looked over at all the dancing and singing fairies and tried to catch a glimpse of her friend Kelly. There, in the middle of the floor and in the midst of a group of swirling green wings and laughing fairies was Kelly. He was whooping and hollering with the rest of them. Ary frantically waved her arms and called his name to get his attention but there were so many waving arms and calling voices that she was easily drowned out. Ary rose up high on her wings and kept waving her arms. Finally, Kelly happened to glance up and see his old friend.

Image 32: Glowing Lights

"Hey! Ary! Blessed Season!" he yelled as he rose above the dancing crowd and moved toward Ary. Together they drifted toward a quieter part of the room. There they landed and embraced.

"Ary? Is that really you? You look... different!" glowed Kelly.

"Different? How?"

"It's...it's your wings! They're... beautiful!"

"Thank you," said Ary unsure of what he had meant. She had been in these dark caverns for weeks and had no opportunity to get a glimpse of her own wings. She had no idea that, over the past few weeks, they had been changing. The light yellow color had transformed into a rich deep yellow and there were lines of differing shades of yellow as well. For now, she only knew that Kelly thought they looked different whether or not they really were different.

"I need your help," she pleaded. "Actually, Scarlet needs your help. Cerise says she's suffering from light deprivation and we need to build her some kind of window."

"A window, huh? That shouldn't be too hard to do. Let me get some help."

Kelly went back to the frolicking crowd and pulled away four other green-winged fairies. They went over to Ary.

"Ok, lets go!" directed Kelly. Ary, Kelly, and the other fairies flew off in the direction of Scarlet and Cerise. Along the way, the green-winged fairies found some twigs they could use for digging. When they arrived, Scarlet was still lying on the floor. When she saw all the other fairies, she rose slightly.

"I think I'm slipping fast!" whined Scarlet.

"Oh, cut it out!" Cerise said to Scarlet pushing her back down to the ground. "You're going to be fine!"

Kelly poked around the dirt above with his stick in the dark. After exploring for a while, he called out to the others.

"I think we can get through over here!" he called out to the others. Though the green-winged fairies were very strong and could push through the dirt with their sticks by themselves, Ary and Scarlet helped as well. After digging and pushing for several moments, they were able to break through the dirt and reached the snow pack from above. Kelly then took a torch and lit it. He used the heat from the flame to just slightly melt the snow while the other green fairies smoothed the snow until it formed a light globe. The light of the sun shone through the snow and ice and created a soft but bright blue glow. All the fairies looked around at the beautiful vision around them. Then, Cerise noticed Ary's wings.

"Ary! Your wings! They're amazing!" she gasped.

Scarlet sat up weakly and said: "Oh my!"

"I told you!" said Kelly.

"Well, thank you, I guess," stammered Ary. "I will just have to take your word for it, though. In the meantime, let's get Scarlet under the light."

All the fairies picked up Scarlet and put her under the new ice window. Scarlet started to feel better almost immediately.

"Thank you all so much!" she exclaimed. "You have saved me!"

"Oh Scarlet!" cried Cerise. "Lay down!"

Scarlet took her friends advice and fell asleep.

"Thank you all so much!" Ary said to Kelly and his friends.

"No problem," responded Kelly. He gathered up his friends and rose up to fly off but turned around to face Ary before leaving. "Will we see you tonight, then?" he asked.

"Tonight?" Ary pondered. She tried to think about what day it was. Then, it came to her. "Oh, yes. It's the Winter Cross-Quarter." She remembered reading about it in one of her books. "Is tonight the Great Lighting?" she asked.

"Why yes!" Kelly answered. "Will you be joining us, then?"

Ary turned toward her two long time friends.

"Go ahead, Ary," said Cerise. "I'll stay here with Scarlet. She'll be just fine. You should really go. It's quite a beautiful ceremony."

Ary turned back to Kelly. "All right, then. I'll be there."

"Great! See you then! Blessed Season!" called Kelly as he and his friends flew off.

Later that night, Ary flew into a large chamber where there were many other fairies of all colors gathered together. They were sitting and chatting quietly while others continued to come in and find places to sit. After a time, the fairies all started to settle down and get quiet. A few of them went around the walls of the large chamber and started to put out the torches. Within a few moments, the hall became pitch dark and completely silent. If Ary hadn't known better she could have believed that she was the only one there in the universe.

She heard the breathing of the other fairies around her and she knew that they were slowly going into a state of meditation. The collective breathing got slower and fuller. Several moments went by but time seemed to stretch into eternity. Ary thought back on her readings about the ceremony. This was the one night that fairies did something very unusual and she would witness it at any moment.

Ary patiently waited and waited. Then, in the midst of the silence came a single droning sound that was soft and low. It started with just one fairy but, little by little, many of the other fairies quietly joined in. Then, it happened. Ary thought she saw it in the distance first but it eventually spread to most of the fairies surrounding her. It was a light glow that actually emanated from deep within each fairy and reflected the color of each of the fairy wings. It was a wonderful and beautiful sight to see this kaleidoscope of gentle lights filling and lighting the room.

Ary knew that each fairy was not able to sustain the luminescence for very long so she watched as long she could. It wasn't long before the lights started to diminish. Soon, the room was black again and a few of the fairies went around the room and re-lit the torches on the walls until the room was full of the familiar yellow-red glow of firelight. Ary looked about and noticed the fairies that were sitting next to her and around her. They all had an air of serene contentment and were smiling gently. It was a very special moment for all those who had participated and watched the ceremony. Eventually, the fairies moved slowly and returned to their places.

Ary decided to head back to her sleeping area but wanted to do one more thing before going to sleep. She flew toward one of the entrances to the caves and stopped at the door that had been constructed there to keep out the cold. She pushed open the door and made her way through the sticks and leaves and had to dig through the snow that was piled up in front of the door. Fortunately, she did not have to work too hard because others had carved a way through before her. It was bitterly cold and Ary knew she had to work fast because she knew that she would not be able to last long in these frigid temperatures. Soon, she was through the snow and flew off to the pond that was just below the frozen waterfall. With her wings she blew the top snow off the water until there remained a clear surface of ice. The moonlight let her see her reflection on the ice. Her friends had been right, her wings were different. Ary took a short moment to admire the colors on her wings and then swiftly returned. She could already feel the cold stiffening her. If she did not return soon she wouldn't be able to fly and risked being stuck out in the cold.

She flew as hard as her stiffening wings could go until she reached the entrance to the tunnel and painfully made her way in. She was nearly frozen stiff when she managed to work her way inside to the warm cave. Just at the entrance Cerise was waiting for her. Ary was shaking from the cold.

"Ary!" cried Cerise as she wrapped her arms around her friend to help her warm up. "You're freezing. When you didn't come back after the ceremony I went asking around to see if anyone knew where you were. Fortunately, a few had seen you go out. I was worried about you."

"How's Scarlet?" Ary managed to say.

"She's fine. Still sleeping," replied Cerise. "Come on. Let's get you back to a warm cot."

With that, the two walked slowly back into the Winter lair.

𝒮𝓉𝑜𝓇𝓎 𝑛𝑜. 16
Good Night

Arylide was a deep golden-winged fairy who lived on a branch of the Great Tree at the edge of the Forest of Songs. These are the stories of her first year.

Image 33: Flower Bud in the Snow

It was late Winter in the Forest of Songs and the fairies, who had been in the underground caves during the Winter, were anxious to get back to living in the Great Tree. Each day around this time of year, several fairies would venture out from the cave entrance and investigate the weather conditions. First, it was reported that the snow was slowly melting. Then, there were reports of slightly warmer days. Finally, came the sighting of grass on the ground. That was the sign the fairies had been hoping to see and it signaled the end of their days in the caves.

On this day, the doors to each of the underground cave entrances were flung wide open and the fairies came flying out into the sunshine.

Ary, Cerise, and Scarlet had been sharing a cramped space together in the caverns and were eager to get back to the Great Tree too so they could have their own spaces again. Ary was especially happy to get back. She had to have all her books packed away in a storage chamber in the fairy lair but now she soon would be able to get them all back to her nest and she could again begin her studies.

The three young fairies flew out of the cave together and took the chance to celebrate. They flew circles and did flips in the air. They flew through branches and around trees and they chased each other around the woods. After a while, they got tired of flying and playing and got to work putting their individual nests back in order. No matter how careful each fairy was to cover and protect their nests, the long Winter always caused the nests to be in disarray come Spring. Ary, Cerise, and Scarlet each went to their own individual nests to begin the spring cleanup.

Ary carefully set all her books and notes back on branch shelves and arranged her nest. Then she set back to enjoy sitting in it again. Since it was not truly Spring, many of the nights would still be very cold and they might have to spend them in the caves but most of the days would allow them chances to come and enjoy the sights and sounds of the outdoors.

It had been nearly a year since Ary had first arrived in the Forest of Songs through the opening of a flower. She thought about all that had happened to her: she recalled all the animals she had met and the friends she and made, she thought about her deeds that she had done to earn her wings and how happy she was to get those wings, she thought about celebrating all the seasonal celebrations and all the adventures she had with her friends, and she thought about all she had learned and how proud she was of her bright yellow wings.

By the end of the day, Ary was exhausted and it was starting to get very cold again. She knew she would have to go back into the caves tonight but wanted to wait until the last possible moment to go in. She flew around the tree and saw the place where she had first arrived. She thought she saw a hint of some flowers trying to push their way through the cold dirt. Soon, other fairies would be brought to the Forest of Songs through the new flowers and Ary knew that she and her friends would help them come into the world. They would teach them about the Forest, about how to earn their wings, about the seasonal celebrations, and about how to relate to other creatures.

Ary flew into the caves and found her friends waiting for her. It had been a long day for all of them so they grabbed something to eat and then went to their cots and readied themselves for sleep. Ary put her head on her pillow of soft leaves and feathers and then whispered good night to her friends. She knew they would all dream of Spring and the beginning of a new year that would be filled with fun and adventure.

16123752R00084

Made in the USA
Lexington, KY
22 July 2012